GARDEN WALLS
FENCES and
HEDGES

GARDEN WALLS
FENCES and
KATHY
SHELDON
HEDGES

 LARK BOOKS

A Division of Sterling Publishing Co., Inc.
New York

Library of Congress Cataloging-in-Publication Data

Sheldon, Kathy, 1959–
   Garden walls, fences, and hedges / Kathy Sheldon.
     p. cm.
   Includes index.
   ISBN 1-57990-211-1 (hardcover) ISBN 1-57990-317-7 (paperback)
   1. Fences—amateurs' manuals. 2. Hedges—amateurs' manuals.
   3. Garden construction—amateurs' manuals. I. Title

   TT4965.S47 2001
   624—dc21   00-05697
                                    CIP

10 9 8 7 6 5 4 3 2 1

Published by Lark Books, a division of
Sterling Publishing Co., Inc.
387 Park Avenue South, New York, N.Y. 10016

© 2001, Lark Books

Distributed in Canada by Sterling Publishing,
c/o Canadian Manda Group, One Atlantic Ave., Suite 105
Toronto, Ontario, Canada M6K 3E7

Distributed in the U.K. by:
Guild of Master Craftsman Publications Ltd.
Castle Place, 166 High Street, Lewes East Sussex, England BN7 1XU
Tel: (+ 44) 1273 477374, Fax: (+ 44) 1273 478606,
Email: pubs@thegmcgroup.com, Web: www.gmcpublications.com

Distributed in Australia by Capricorn Link (Australia) Pty Ltd., P.O. Box 704, Windsor,
NSW 2756 Australia

Every effort has been made to ensure that all the information in this book is accurate.
However, due to differing conditions, tools, and individual skills, the publisher cannot be
responsible for any injuries, losses, and other damages that may result from the use of the
information in this book.

If you have questions or comments about this book, please contact:
Lark Books
67 Broadway
Asheville, NC 28801
(828) 236-9730

Manufactured in China

ISBN 1-57990-211-1 (hardcover) ISBN 1-57990-317-7 (paperback)

CHRIS BRYANT
art director

DON OSBY
illustrator

RICHARD FREUDENBERGER
technical consultant

HANNES CHAREN
production assistant

VERONIKA ALICE GUNTER
editorial assitant

EMMA JONES
ROPER CLELAND
interns

DEREK FELL
cover photograph

Contents

introduction

I CAN STILL REMEMBER MY FIRST AFTERNOON as a homeowner. I opened the front door with the key I'd been given at the closing (a skeleton key that fit into a lock installed when the house was built in 1926) and walked through the bungalow surveying layers of wallpaper to tear down and square feet of shag carpet to pull up, thinking, *mine*. Then I walked out into the tiny backyard, overgrown with brush and blackberry canes, and I realized with a start that I owned, not just a house, but a piece of land—a little patch of the planet.

I had the immediate, overwhelming desire to enclose the yard and begin the process of turning the space into my private paradise. I could imagine a fence covered with blossoming vines along the street side (not too tall a fence, since I'm nosey), a dense hedge along the back (to hide the neighbor's rusting appliances), and a stone retaining wall on a sloped section that would allow me a few more precious feet of level ground.

Humans first built borders for protection, of course (back when the shaggy things that scared us were wild beasts and invaders instead of carpeting). Borders have also been used for centuries to mark boundaries and to provide privacy and shelter. The words *garden* and *yard* both trace their ancestry to a word meaning enclosure. The word *paradise* comes from the Persian word for a walled garden.

Today, a wall, fence, or hedge can still fulfill all these functions while it transforms the look of your yard or garden. In fact, a border is likely to have more of an impact on your yard's appearance than any other single element. Unfortunately, it's also the element that typically has the largest impact on your budget. In the pages that follow, you'll learn how to get the most for your money and labor by finding a border that increases both the value and the beauty of your home.

The first chapter of this book presents all the functions various borders can perform—some that may already be on your wish list and some that you'll want to add. This is followed by information you'll need to evaluate your specific site, and then a look at other considerations (including legal ones) to help you avoid making costly mistakes.

The individual chapters on walls, fences, and hedges examine each category of border in depth, and offer criteria for choosing a border that will most meet your needs. Would a board or a lattice fence work best for you? Are you tempted by the crisp lines (but rather demanding maintenance needs) of a formal hedge, or would an informal hedge be more appropriate for your site? You'll find dozens of gorgeous photos of different types of borders to inspire you and help narrow your search. If you choose a border that calls for the skills and equipment of a professional, the information here will insure that you get the most for your money. In addition, detailed instructions and illustrations are provided for making several borders, ranging from somewhat challenging (a picket fence or low brick wall) to downright simple (a sunflower border).

Once your new wall, fence, or hedge goes up, the fun begins. The tempting photographs and practical instructions in the chapter on plants and borders will have you grabbing your spade in no time. The whimsical ideas for enhancing borders, found in the final chapter, are certain to bring out the artist in you and help you make your border look at home, no matter where home may be. In fact, it matters little whether the space you'll be enclosing is a small city garden, a suburban backyard, or a rolling rural expanse—surround it with the right wall, fence, or hedge, and it will become your own version of paradise.

Function and Design

THOSE OF US WHO ENJOY WORKING IN OUR YARDS and gardens are usually habitual rearrangers. One year we want the purple iris smack dab in front of the pink peony. Two years later we start to wonder how that iris's upright, swordlike foliage would look beside the hosta's heart-shaped leaves. We also tend to be just a bit impulsive. Admit it: how many unopened seed packets do you have lying around the house? But moving a 5-foot-high brick wall just a tad to the left is not the same as transplanting a clump of asters, and figuring out what to do with fifteen 1-gallon boxwoods is not the same as squeezing in one more variety of daylily.

A border—whether it's a wall, fence, or hedge—usually requires a sizable investment in time and money. Chances are, your choice will still be standing when it's time to sell your home. Build or plant one with care, and it may still be standing long after you no longer can! So it's important to clarify in advance exactly *why* and *where* you want a border. Then you'll need to consider the conditions of your specific site, any legal restrictions, and the costs (both long- and short-term).

Functions

Perhaps you already know exactly why you want a border. You'd like to block the noise and pollution from a busy street, or you're tired of watching your neighbor's compulsive Saturday afternoon car washing (who can enjoy a good snooze in the hammock with all that work going on?). Maybe you're trying to prevent intruders from breaking into your property or your golden retriever with wanderlust from breaking out. Or perhaps your goal is less practical: you crave climbing roses intertwined with clematis, and you need a structure for them to scramble up and over.

Before you rush out and build or plant the wall, fence, or hedge that suits your purpose, stop and think. Most borders can (and will) serve more than one function. Often this is a bonus: the fence that provides security could, if designed right, create the perfect microclimate for growing plants that normally won't survive in your zone. Sometimes, though, this creates a problem—the tall, solid wall that provides absolute privacy might also cast shade and funnel wind gusts right onto your patio.

When I surrounded my backyard with a lattice-topped board fence several years ago, I knew my goals were privacy and keeping my then-toddler from toddling out into the street. I paid no attention to the 6-inch gap between the bottom of the fence and the ground. Paid no attention until a year later when we adopted a small terrier that managed to squeeze through that gap each time she spotted a squirrel on the other side. This is why you should get out your crystal ball and try to look into the future well before you start to build or plant. Right now you may not mind gazing over a picket fence at the cute little boy riding his tricycle next door. But a few years down the road when he turns 16 and trades in the trike for a motorcycle, you may wish you'd chosen a more sight- and soundproof barrier.

DIVIDING AND DEFINING SPACE

Marking a boundary is perhaps the most common function of a wall, fence, or hedge. We place them around the perimeter of properties to show, both physically and psychologically, what "belongs" to us—to separate private space from public space. On a more practical level, a boundary can establish where your yard ends and the neighbor's begins, or it can encourage visitors to use the path instead of shortcutting across your grass.

But walls, fences, and hedges also play important roles within a yard or garden. Here they can create outdoor rooms, distinct areas with separate functions, not unlike the rooms in your home. Again, this can be largely psychological (a hedge around a patio might lend a feeling of peace and seclusion) or practical (a metal fence can make a swimming pool safer).

Enclosing a large yard will help give it definition and make it feel cozier. Surprisingly, enclosing a small yard can make it feel larger, especially if you take care not to use a very high border that makes the space feel claustrophobic. Divide a small space so that every aspect can't be taken in with a single glance, and it will suddenly feel more expansive. Screening off sections of a small garden creates a sense of mystery that invites people to explore what's around the next corner.

PRIVACY

How comfortable would you feel inside your home if it had no walls? Dining outside with family and friends, lounging on the chaise, and even assuming those unflattering weeding positions are all more relaxing when you feel a sense of privacy. Unfortunately, many houses in the suburbs, on city lots, or in new developments have yards that run right up against each other. No matter how fond you are of your neighbors, you probably don't want them to witness your every successful (or unsuccessful) flip of a burger.

This doesn't mean that you need to surround yourself with solid, 10-foot-high walls just to feel at ease in your yard or garden. In fact, most communities have zoning or building regulations that restrict the height of fences and walls. Structures that aren't completely solid can provide a sense of privacy while maintaining the feeling of openness that brings us outdoors in the first place. Consider using a tall, free-standing section of a fairly solid wall, fence, or planting where privacy is most desired—beside a patio or hot tub, for example—while choosing a more open design to enclose the rest of your yard. A row of tall, ornamental grasses or a hedge of tall annuals can provide inexpensive privacy (and shade) for a part of your yard you're apt to use only in warm weather.

As a general rule, your boundary will give you the greatest sense of privacy if it is eye level or higher, so you can't see over it. But remember, the farther away from the structure or planting you get, the easier it will be to see over it, so go to the far edge of your yard to determine an adequate boundary height. If privacy is your top priority, you may also want to situate your border to block views into your house from the street or the neighbors' yards.

OPPOSITE PAGE, TOP: This brick wall creates a cozy private enclave yet offers an enticing view of the gardens beyond.

OPPOSITE PAGE, BOTTOM: Picket fences can keep children out of flower beds but still safely in sight.

LEFT: Privacy fences need not be completely solid.

SECURITY

Deterrence and containment were the original functions of walls, fences, and hedges. Keeping invaders and wild animals out and preventing domestic animals from wandering off or destroying crops were once crucial to human survival. Even if marauders and hungry beasts no longer pose a threat, keeping your family safe may still be a priority.

For a structure to provide security, it must be tall, solid, and difficult to climb over or under. A wall or fence that is 6 feet high or higher will usually discourage all but the most determined climbers. Choosing a design that eliminates handholds and footholds is also important. Fences made from stakes and palings are descendants of early palisade walls, and their design principles still hold true: pointed tops, such as pickets or the spikes of an iron fence, make scaling a structure difficult. (More drastic measures— such as razor wire, embedded glass, or electric wire—are illegal in many communities.) If the top of a fence is not pointed, then make sure it has an extra wide cap on top so it doesn't provide an easy handgrip.

Of course, the most secure fence or wall is useless against intruders if its gate or door is easy to break through, so these features also must be designed with security in mind. Padlocks, inside latches, and remote control locks are all options, depending on where the gate or door is located and how it's typically used.

If the main function of your boundary is keeping four-legged intruders out of your garden, make it tall and hard to squeeze through or

This brick wall enhances the appearance of the yard it surrounds, but it also presents a formidable barrier to intruders.

burrow under. (Boards, such as 2 x 8s or thin walls of concrete, set 2 inches from a fence bottom should discourage burrowing. But don't allow contact between the boards or concrete and the bottom of a wooden fence, or the fence may begin to rot.)

All sorts of boundaries have been erected in attempts to keep deer out of gardens—most have been unsuccessful. Deer can jump fences that are 10 feet high, but their favored method is to push through or under fencing. Electrical fencing is an option not covered in this book; otherwise, you might try a wire fence at least 8 feet tall, with the wires in the bottom 4 feet of fence no more than 10 inches apart.

If your goal is not keeping wild animals out, but rather keeping pets and wild children *in*, your wall or fence design will depend on your specific needs. (Hedges are generally unsuitable for this purpose, since their bottoms offer a passageway out, but a low-growing thorny one might work.) To confine a dog, a wall or fence needs to be at least 5 feet high (higher for a very large dog). Metal fences are often preferred by dog owners since they are not as easily scratched or chewed as wood. Cats can usually be kept in by a solid barrier that is at least 4 feet high, but it must be one they can't climb up and over. Walls and fences built to keep children in the yard should be 5 to 6 feet tall, with no footholds or handholds to offer temptation.

Requirements for fences or walls surrounding swimming pools are often mandated by local zoning regulations and insurance policies. Check these carefully, so you can be sure the design you have in mind will be in full compliance.

TOP: The wire mesh added to this post-and-rail fence would be enough to keep toddlers or some small pets safely contained.

BOTTOM: Securely enclosing a swimming pool is not only common sense—in most places it's required by law.

TEMPERING THE ENVIRONMENT

Perhaps your favorite plant thrives in just one USDA zone to the south, but your spouse can't see the logic of relocating the entire family for the sake of a tender perennial. Or you positioned your patio to catch the evening breeze, but now all your outdoor meals have turned into a game of "catch the paper plates." Or maybe that steady swish of traffic the realtor swore "you could hardly hear" has begun to make relaxing outside feel more like torture. Properly de-signed and located, walls, fences, and hedges can create microclimates conducive to the plants you wish to grow, add both sun and shade to your garden, buffer strong winds, and muffle noise.

Garden dividers almost always have one sunny side and one shady side. Take advantage of this to grow a variety of plants. Plants that languish in the glare of the afternoon sun will welcome the shade cast by a nearby wall, fence, or hedge. Grow full-sun plants that prefer a milder climate than your garden normally provides on the south side of walls or fences that you've painted a light color and oriented east to west. The struc-ture will absorb solar heat through-out the day and then release it during the night.

If your yard or garden is battered by winds, you might be tempted to erect a solid barrier to serve as a windbreak, but this will actually exacerbate the problem. As shown

An open brick wall can buffer winds and create a more temperate microclimate for plants.

Hedges can buffer both noise and wind gusts. Unlike walls and fences, they are usually exempt from height restrictions.

in figure 1, the lee side of a solid structure often suffers from downdrafts and strong gusts, since the wind vaults right up and over the fence or wall. Open designs (such as figure 2), which allow the wind to permeate the barrier, do a much better job of slowing down the wind while providing air circulation that will benefit both you and your plants.

Solid barriers, on the other hand, are most effective at buffering noise. The best sound barrier is a thick wall at least 6 feet tall; sound waves will bounce off the structure most readily if it has a smooth surface. Alternatively, fairly solid, rough-textured fences or dense hedges can absorb sound if they are tall enough. What should you do if you live near a noisy street but also have a windy yard or if local regulations limit the height of your structure? Then you probably are best off with a hedge (for which there usually are no height restrictions) or a fence or wall with a fairly open design. Simply obstructing the view to the source of the noise can help make it less noticeable.

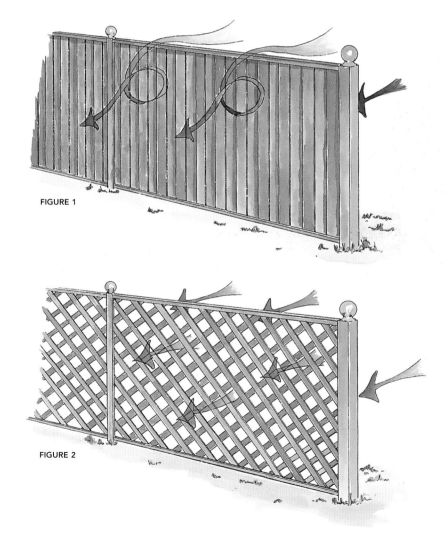

FIGURE 1

FIGURE 2

A sloped section of yard can be transformed into useful space with the help of a stone retaining wall.

CREATING LEVEL AREAS

Mowing a steep lawn can be dangerous, lounging or dining on one is inconvenient, and playing croquet up and down one, just about impossible. Sloped ground is difficult to garden because the soil (which is subject to erosion) tends to be dry and to lack nutrients. But a retaining wall can change all that. With a wall to hold back the earth, you can create level areas in your yard for a flower bed, a small patio, and—if not a croquet court—maybe at least a place to play fetch with something other than a billy goat.

The forces on retaining walls are considerable, and adequate drainage is essential, so careful design and construction are of vital importance here. Walls more than 3- to 4-feet high are usually subject to building codes and should be built by a professional. Materials suitable for a retaining wall—depending on the wall's height and the amount of soil it will be retaining—include stone, brick, concrete block, interlocking concrete blocks, and landscape timbers.

DECORATION

Just as with people, there are borders among us that do not actually have to work for a living; they just need to look good. Nobody asks them to keep the dog out of the traffic, no one demands that they block an unsightly view or buffer the wind or create a microclimate. Staying gorgeous—maintaining an erect, well-pruned, uncracked, and unblistered appearance—is their full-time job.

Of course, what most of us want is a wall, fence, or hedge that performs a function or two and looks good at the same time. Getting this is really just a matter of keeping aesthetics in mind when determining the design, height, and placement of your border. Be sure the wall surface that deflects sound is also attractive. Make certain the hedge you plant for privacy has foliage you admire. Compromises will have to be made, but a quick look through this book should assure you of the many hardworking borders out there that manage to do their jobs and still look beautiful.

Beauty and function have found the perfect balance in this garden's decorative border.

Evaluating Your Site

Now that you know *what* you want your border to do, it's time to decide *where* to locate it. This will depend in part on the functions the border will serve, but it will also depend on the specifics of your particular site.

STEP OUTSIDE

The time has come to step outside and look around. As you examine your site, keep the following factors in mind. They will all play a role in determining the type of border you choose and where to locate it.

■ How you currently use the different parts of your yard; how you hope to use them in the future. The current flow of foot traffic. Where openings in a wall, fence, or hedge need to be located and how wide those openings should be.

■ Views out from your property you'd like to conceal and views you'd like to retain and perhaps even emphasize.

■ Views into your property you'd like to block (remember this may include windows or doors that afford a view into your house) and features you'd like to have remain in view or perhaps even emphasize.

■ The source of any bothersome noise you'd like to muffle.

■ Obstacles (trees, rock outcrops, buildings, etc.) that may be in the way of your wall, fence, or hedge. (Remember that borders do not have to be designed in straight lines and can often be built or planted around such obstacles.)

■ The prevailing wind direction on your site.

■ The path of the sun across your property (this will, of course, vary throughout the year). The sections of yard or garden you'd like to have remain sunny and those where you could use more shade.

■ The topography of your site. How steep are the slopes? Any low-lying areas?

■ The current drainage patterns. Are there any drainage problems?

■ The soil conditions in various parts of your yard or garden. (This affects how you build foundations for walls and set posts for fences, as well as the type of hedges you can grow.)

Other Considerations

Once you've determined the specific needs of your particular site, you still have a few more important questions to ask before you start mixing mortar or digging postholes—questions such as "is it legal?" and "can I afford it?"

LEGAL ASPECTS

In many communities, zoning regulations or subdivision bylaws restrict the size, placement, and even the style of a wall or fence (hedges are generally not regulated), so be sure to check these thoroughly before getting started. Depending on your project, local building codes may also apply to the design and construction of your fence or wall.

Good fences may make good neighbors, but if the location of your fence is off by even an inch or two, you may be too good of a neighbor— you will have just built a fence that doesn't belong to you! You must know the exact location of your property lines before you plant a hedge or build a fence or wall. The cost of hiring a surveyor to find and mark the property lines and file an official record will certainly be cheaper than tearing down and rebuilding a structure. If the original survey stakes are still in place, get your neighbors to sign a document agreeing to their location.

If your fence, wall, or hedge straddles the property line, then your neighbors legally own the half that is in their yard and are entitled to do whatever they like with it. They could paint their side of a fence hot pink or prune topiary flying pigs atop their half of a hedge. You could get your neighbors to sign a document that states that each neighbor agrees to maintain the wall, fence, or

Check on setback requirements and easements before building or planting beside a road.

hedge in a certain manner, but remember, new owners may not agree to the arrangement. Your safest bet is to build or plant your border at least 6 inches in from the property line. Remember, too, it is sometimes the law and usually the custom to build fences so that the "good side" (the board side) faces your neighbor's property while the frame side faces in. You can avoid this by choosing a "good neighbor" design that is finished on both sides.

Another legal consideration is the issue of easements. Sometimes utility companies have easements that allow them access to your yard. If this is the case, you may still be able to enclose your property, but you will have to provide a gate for access. Information about these should be on your deed, but you'll have to

check with local utility companies to be certain. If you're building or planting beside a road, check with the highway department to find out about any setback requirements.

UNDERGROUND UTILITIES

Never, ever dig a hole in your yard without being certain of the exact location and depth of any underground utilities. Severing a power or gas line could be extremely costly or even fatal. Most local utility companies are happy to locate underground lines on your property for free. You can also hire a company that specializes in finding underground utilities (listed in your phone book's business section under "Utilities Underground Cable, Pipe & Wire Locating Service").

This fence and arbor harmonize perfectly with the house by borrowing architectural details from the structure.

STYLE AND SCALE

The style of your house or garden should influence the type of boundary you choose. A bamboo fence would appear out of place in front of a Victorian but at home with the simple lines of a contemporary house on the California coast. A formal hedge would probably look pretentious in front of a suburban ranch house where a split rail might better fit the bill, but that same hedge would be just right enclosing the formal gardens of a Colonial brick home.

Scale also needs to be considered. A small bungalow can easily be dwarfed by a huge front wall while a short fence will look silly surrounding a large property. Once you've decided on the dimensions you need your wall, fence, or hedge to be in order to perform the jobs you've prioritized, then make sure its size will be in scale with its surroundings.

COST

Far be it from me to be the party pooper here, but somewhere along the line—hopefully sooner rather than later—you'll need to ask yourself what the project you have in mind will cost. When you do so, remember all the hidden expenses: gates, hardware, and finishes for fences; foundation materials and mortar for walls. Even a hedge, which can be fairly inexpensive if you're patient and start it with small plants, may be costly to maintain if you lack the time or physical ability to prune it yourself.

If budget constraints keep you from erecting the wall, fence, or hedge of your dreams right away, plan your project in stages. You might put up less costly chain-link fencing right now just to keep your pets and children safe, while you save for an expensive wooden fence you covet or start building a brick wall as time and finances allow. Likewise, if you can't afford large plants for a hedge but want privacy right away, plant a row of sunflowers or some other tall annual beside very small hedge plants.

In general, walls tend to be the most expensive to build initially, but they also, if constructed with care, can last the longest and cost little to maintain. Fences, especially wooden ones, while less expensive to build, usually require regular maintenance and eventually will need to be replaced. The initial cost of a hedge varies widely depending on the type and age of the plants used. Formal hedges can be time-consuming to maintain (and let's face it, time is money for most of us); informal hedges require less care. Remember, too, that when you plant a hedge you're dealing with a living thing, so you're always taking a bit of a gamble in terms of life expectancy. Tip the odds in your favor by choosing healthy plants of a variety that's reliable in your climate and soil conditions. It only makes sound economic sense to use the strongest (or, in the case of plants, healthiest) materials you can afford. Flimsy lattice that needs to be replaced after a few years can end up being costly. And bargain privet plants that die in a matter of months are no bargain.

ABOVE: Even inexpensive, temporary fencing can be cheerful.

BELOW, LEFT: Sunflowers can serve as a seasonal border while young hedge plants become established.

BELOW, RIGHT: Chain-link fences can be made more attractive with plantings, such as this vigorous trumpet vine.

chapter

2 Walls

THINK *WALLS* AND YOU MAY envision the exotic, tiled structures enclosing Persian gardens or the humble but handsome stone walls crisscrossing New England. Despite the fact that walls come in so many different styles, they're generally divided into only three main categories, based on the material used: brick, stone, or concrete (timber is sometimes used for retaining walls). Typically the most permanent of garden boundaries, freestanding walls are also usually the most expensive to build or have built. However, a well-constructed wall will last for many years and will require considerably less maintenance than most fences or hedges.

Walls are usually the most solid of the three borders types—if your main priority is blocking noise or creating privacy or security, a tall wall may be the right choice. No other border is as effective at making a garden feel separate from the world outside. Walls can also be the most versatile of borders. Features such as seating, barbecues, outdoor fireplaces, fountains, and planters can all be incorporated right into the structures. With the information from the first chapter in mind, let the guide that follows help you narrow your search for the best border for you.

ABOVE, RIGHT: Many fields enclosed by old dry-stack stone walls have reverted back to forest.

Dry Stone

New England is home to many dry-stacked stone walls a couple of hundred years old, but in parts of Europe dry-stacked walls can be found that date back to the Bronze Age. Such permanence is only part of the appeal of stone walls. They are attractive, they are hardworking, and they bespeak the value of careful, time-consuming craftsmanship.

Extremely labor-intensive to build, dry stone walls rely on gravity rather than mortar to stay in place. Fitting the pieces together is something akin to completing a very challenging (and heavy!) jigsaw puzzle. But while they

are time-consuming to build, these walls don't require a lot in the way of tools or materials. Unlike mortared walls, dry-stacked stone walls can shift slightly to accommodate the movement of the soil below, and so usually require only foundations of hard-packed earth and gravel.

Because these walls cannot be built very high, they provide little in the way of privacy or security. Dry-stacked stone retaining walls are excellent at holding back low banks and providing a microclimate for plants. Freestanding dry-stacked stone walls—built mainly for their good looks these days—are effective at defining boundaries.

Mortared Stone

When mortar is used to hold stone walls together, the wall can be built higher and so put to more uses. Mortared walls can vary widely in their appearance, depending on both their structure and the type of stone used. Stone that's been carefully cut to uniform shape and size is referred to as *dressed stone* or *ashlar*. Uncut stone is called *fieldstone* or *rubble*. In general, mortared walls built from dressed stone will look more formal and will cost more than walls built from fieldstone. In either case, local stone will usually look best with your landscape and will cost less than stone that has to be transported from a distance. How the mortar holding the stones together is finished, or *pointed,* will also affect the appearance of the wall.

Mortared walls require concrete footings and the careful construction that must usually be provided by a stone mason. These can be among the most expensive of all borders, but a well-built mortared stone wall is also apt to be the most permanent border money can buy. And you can get a lot for your money—this type of wall can, depending on its height, fulfill just about every function you could ask of a border. About the only thing a mortared stone wall can't do is provide a windscreen, but a structure consisting of stone columns with lattice infill can make an attractive border that will effectively buffer strong winds without creating downdrafts.

Although it is only a couple of years old, this mortared stone wall looks as though it could have been in place for centuries.

This beautifully patinaed wall shows how gracefully brick can age.

Brick

Essentially baked blocks of pressed clay, bricks are one of our oldest construction materials. The fact that they are still in use is testimony to the way these low-tech blocks can be transformed into a diverse array of wall styles, from intimidating, fortress-like barriers to sensuously undulating serpentine structures to open, airy screens.

The color of clay, and thus the appearance of bricks, differs from one location to another; bricks manufactured locally are apt to fit in well with your landscape. Weathered bricks tend to blend in better with plants than new ones, and they have the added advantage of making your garden look as if it has been around for years. (Whatever bricks you use, make sure they are the correct grade for your climate.) The appearance of a brick wall will also be determined by the bond pattern used to lay the bricks, the thickness of the wall, the pointing of the mortar that holds the bricks together, and the method used to cap the wall to deflect rainwater.

Brick walls up to 3 feet high on fairly level ground can be tackled by a homeowner; anything higher requires the design and construction expertise of a bricklayer. Although low brick walls can be built just one brick thick (these are referred to as *single-wythe* walls), a two-brick-thick (*double-wythe*) wall will be much stronger and will last much longer. Bricks themselves are fairly inexpensive, but the actual cost of a brick wall can vary, depending on the size of the structure, the design, and whether or not the services of an expert are required.

Low brick walls are useful as boundaries within a garden, as retaining walls on slopes, or as a divider at the edge of a patio. Tall brick walls are excellent for privacy and security, for reducing the noise and dirt from traffic, for creating warm microclimates for plants, and for keeping pets and children constrained. (Rumor has it that they can even keep big, bad wolves at bay.) Open brick walls can be effective as windscreens; tall, solid brick walls create downdrafts. A tall, solid brick wall will also cast shade in the garden, which may or may not be a benefit.

Concrete

Concrete walls are valued because they're strong, relatively inexpensive, and they go up quickly. What many people don't realize is that concrete walls can also be beautiful. Finished with a coat of stucco, a concrete wall can mimic adobe or finely dressed stone. The flat surface of a concrete wall makes the perfect canvas for decorative touches such as mosaics or murals.

Concrete blocks are one of the most user-friendly materials for walls. The challenge is not in the building process, but rather in muscling the heavy blocks (which typically weigh 40 to 45 pounds each) into place. Cinder blocks, composed of lighter material, weigh (and cost) considerably less, but they are also not as strong as standard concrete block (their use is often restricted by local building codes).

A *poured* or *in situ* concrete wall, on the other hand, is *not* a project for a beginner. To make these walls (which may be curved or straight), concrete with steel reinforcing wire is cast in a form, usually made from plywood. These walls can be especially striking with contemporary architecture and in urban gardens.

Depending on their height and construction, concrete walls, whether poured or constructed from blocks, can fulfill just about any function. As with all solid borders, though, they can create wind gusts. Unfortunately, most of the decorative concrete screen blocks available look dated and out of place in a garden setting.

ABOVE: Even a ho-hum concrete wall can become a vibrant land-scape accent with a bright coat of paint.

RIGHT: With the right finish, concrete can fit in with almost any setting.

LEFT: This long, steep slope is held in check with interlocking concrete blocks.

BELOW: Because they handle curves easily, interlocking concrete blocks are often used to edge planting beds.

Interlocking Concrete Retaining Systems

Concrete wall systems offer one of the easiest methods for building a retaining wall. These walls get their strength from modular blocks that use various mechanisms to interlock with one another without mortar. The blocks come in many different colors and shapes (some are hollow inside and can be planted) and can be stacked into straight or curved walls. These systems are for retaining walls, so while they work well for creating level areas, they usually won't provide privacy or security.

Plants can help timber retaining walls blend in with their surroundings.

Timber

Landscape timber retaining walls are practical walls. They get the job done without a whole lot of fuss or expense. They won't last as long as a stone wall, but if you use pressure-treated timbers, they could, depending on soil conditions, last for a few decades. Railroad ties are *not* recommended; they're saturated with creosote (which is toxic), they're difficult to work with, and they're also usually ugly.

Most landscape timber walls consist of stacked timbers that use a system of *deadmen* (perpendicular timbers embedded in the bank) for stability. A concrete footing is usually unnecessary. These walls, like most retaining walls, are limited in the functions they can serve in your yard or garden.

Ha-Ha

Okay, okay, so you don't own a manor house with exquisite views of a private park. But if you *did*, wouldn't it be fun to say to your guests, "Let us take a stroll to gaze out beyond the ha-ha."? Popular in 18th-century Britain, ha-has were a landscaping device that employed ditches and retaining walls—invisible from the house—to keep animals contained while maintaining the view and the appearance of an uninterrupted expanse of lawn. Not terribly practical these days, when fewer of us own manors or have livestock grazing our lawns, ha-has are expensive to build and need to be designed carefully to avoid drainage problems. If the illusion works too well, they could also pose a hazard to unsuspecting guests, who may find the sudden drop of a ha-ha less than amusing.

Ha-has were used to keep livestock off lawns without hindering the view.

Building Wall Footings

THE SOIL BENEATH A WALL WILL SINK and shift and (in areas with very cold winters) even heave. When this happens beneath a wall held rigid with mortar, the wall can crack or collapse. A concrete footing, which provides a solid barrier between the wall and the soil, helps prevent this from happening. Whether or not you need a footing (and the type of footing required) depends on the design and height of the wall and the climate and soil conditions of your site. Your local building inspections department can give you advice for your specific area—including whether or not a permit is required—but the following instructions should serve for most mortared walls 3 feet or less in height that are constructed on fairly level ground. Seek the advice of a professional if your wall will run on a slope; sloped walls require special stepped footings.

INSTRUCTIONS

1 First, determine the size footing your intended wall requires. Footings usually need to be twice as wide as the walls they support, with their length extending at least 4 inches beyond the ends of the wall. As a general rule, the footing's thickness should equal the wall's width. In severe winter climates, footing excavations need to extend below the frost line to prevent frost heave. When you check with your local building inspections department, you can find out how deep you need to dig footings in your area.

2 Drive 1 x 2 stakes into the ground to mark the four corners of the intended wall. Stretch mason's line between the stakes to outline the edges of the footing.

3 Unless the excavation is particularly deep because of frost concerns, you can dig the footing trench with a flat-bladed spade and, if needed, a mattock. The depth must take into account not only the thickness of the footing, but any gravel you might use as a subbase in unstable soils. When digging, take care not to disturb any soil beyond what you need to remove to complete the trench. Square the sides and level the bottom of the trench with the spade.

4 To insure that the bottom is level, periodically lay a 2 x 4 across the trench opening and measure to the bottom with a measuring tape. Or you can nail a piece of plywood onto the 2 x 4 so that the plywood extends to the correct trench depth. Then lay the 2 x 4 across the top of the trench, making sure the bottom of the plywood is snug against the trench bottom, as shown in figure 1. If you should collapse the side of the trench at any point, install temporary form boards against stable soil and secure them with stakes to prevent the concrete from slumping.

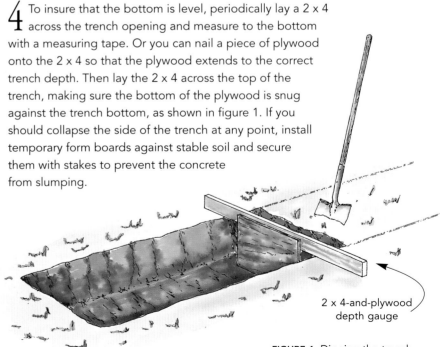

2 x 4-and-plywood depth gauge

FIGURE 1. Digging the trench

FIGURE 2. Pouring the concrete

5 Remove any loose soil from the trench and tamp the bottom. Check the base of the trench with a carpenter's level, or for longer runs, level a mason's line over the length of the trench between the batter boards and measure down from that. In unstable soil (or soil subject to frost heave), lay a 4- to 6-inch sub-base of ¾-inch gravel in the bottom of the trench. Rake it level, tamp the gravel firmly over the length of the trench, and check for level once again.

6 Use a sledgehammer to drive 2-foot lengths of reinforcing bar, "rebar," every 4 feet down the center of the trench. These will serve as the "grade pegs" you will use later to mark and level the top of the concrete, so the aboveground part of the rebar should equal the depth of your concrete footing.

7 Calculate the quantity of concrete you'll need for the job by measuring (in feet) the length, width, and depth of the trench and multiplying the figures to arrive at a cubic-foot measure. A 12-foot by 16-inch by 4-inch trench would be calculated as 12 x 1⅓ x ⅓, or 5¼ cubic feet. For small jobs, 60-pound bags of pre-mixed concrete are most convenient. This 5¼ cubic foot (or 16 square foot, with 4-inch depth) project would require 11 bags of mix; if the depth were 6 inches (making 8 cubic feet), it would need 16 bags. Your builder's supply or home center should have a chart that will allow you to calculate quantities based on your square footage needs. If the job is large enough, you might consider having ready-mix concrete delivered, but be prepared to pay a premium for delivery of small quantities.

8 Before mixing and pouring concrete, get some work gloves and safety glasses (cement is caustic); then enlist the aid of a helper, and clear the work area of any debris that will prevent clear access to any part of the trench. Use a wheelbarrow or mortar box and a mixing hoe to blend water with the concrete mix. Don't work with too much material in one batch, and add water sparingly as you mix—your goal is to make a plastic, nearly fluid mixture, not a soupy or watery one. Starting at one end of the trench, pour the concrete, as shown in figure 2, and move it with a shovel to prevent it from mounding in one spot. Spread it evenly with successive pours, and keep the height below or at the imbedded rebar pins as you move. Work the mix into the corners and eliminate any air pockets with slicing movements of your shovel.

9 Once the trench is filled, use a scrap of 2 x 4 cut to the appropriate length to screed the surface of the footing level with the tops of the rebar grade pegs. Work in a zigzag motion, as shown in figure 3, from one end to the other to knock down high spots and fill in voids at the surface. This action also helps the concrete to set up properly, and provides a slightly rough surface for a good mortar bond later.

10 Leave the stakes and batter boards set up—you'll use them again when you construct a wall on top of the footing. Clean your tools and equipment thoroughly with cold water when you're finished. The concrete will set up in an hour or so, but will not cure to sufficient strength for a few days. To prevent cracking during this period, the concrete must be kept moist. Spray the footing with water a few times each day and keep it covered with plastic. Wait at least a week before beginning any construction work on top of the footing.

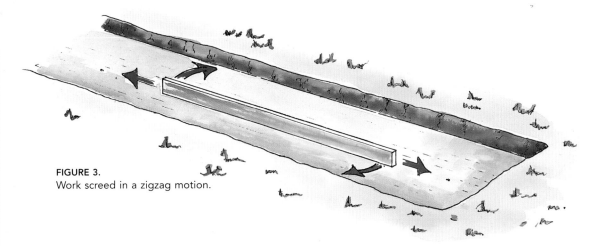

FIGURE 3.
Work screed in a zigzag motion.

A Low Brick Wall

Constructing your own brick wall may seem like a formidable task, but once you get the hang of it, building a low brick wall is surprisingly easy. Such walls can serve as interior boundaries in your yard—enclosing a patio, perhaps—or they can separate your front yard from the street. Instructions for building a concrete footing for a low brick wall can be found on page 30. You'll need to allow at least a week between building the footing and laying up the wall so the concrete has time to cure completely.

MATERIALS

Bricks (see Tips)

Mortar

2 x 4, 16 inches long

1 x 4, 3 feet long

TOOLS AND SUPPLIES

4 stakes (1 x 2s would work well)

Mason's line

Tape measure

Line level

Wheelbarrow or mortar box
  (see step 2)

Hoe

Brick and pointing trowels

Carpenter's level

Joint tool

Pencil (or black pen)

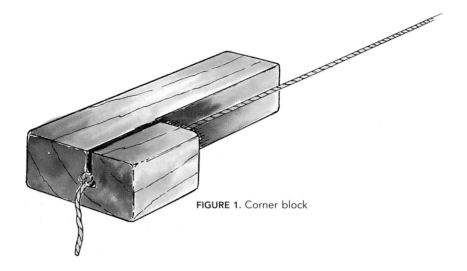

FIGURE 1. Corner block

TIPS

■ Before beginning this project, check with officials about local building codes; they may dictate minimum specifications for a brick wall in your area.

■ You'll probably be working with common brick in a 3½- x 7½- x 2¼-inch size, give or take a fraction. Count on using about 60 bricks for every face square yard of wall, and make sure you purchase brick that's graded for your climate. Make sure you have two solid bricks to put at either end of the capping on the top of the wall.

■ Bricks should be slightly damp when you lay them; otherwise, they'll steal moisture from the mortar joint. Spray them down an hour or so before using them, so they'll be damp, not dripping wet, when you lay them.

■ Corner blocks and mason's string are used as a guide to keep each course of brick level. To make two corner blocks, first use the handsaw to cut the 16-inch 2 x 4 in half. Then cut a 4-inch x 1¾-inch rectangle out of one corner of each 8-inch block (see figure 1). Cut a slot into the middle of the uncut section of each block. Wrap mason's line around this end of each block, securing it in the slot.

■ Use a story pole to check the height of each course as you proceed. Make one by marking a 3-foot 1 x 4 with lines that indicate one brick plus a ½-inch mortar joint. Hold the story pole upright against the wall as you work to check the top of each course.

INSTRUCTIONS

1 Use the stakes and mason's line to mark the outline of the wall, directly over the center of the cured footing. The distance between the two strings (which will match the width of the brick wall) should be equal to the length of one brick. This will equal the width of two bricks plus a ½-inch mortar joint. The lines must be perfectly parallel and about 2 inches above the top of the footing. Lay a "dry run" of two rows of brick on the footing, setting each brick lengthwise against one string and leaving a ½-inch space between each brick, both at the ends and along the sides. Use the carpenter's level to check the tops of the rows, then mark the position of each brick directly onto the foundation. Remove the bricks.

2 Use the hoe to mix your mortar in a wheelbarrow or mortar box, starting with small amounts if you have no experience laying brick. A 60-pound bag of dry, premixed mortar will yield about ½ cubic foot of workable mortar when properly mixed. The mixture should be moist and firm, not soupy. Use the brick trowel to spread an even ⅝-inch layer of mortar within the marked chalk lines on the footing, then furrow the bed with the tip of the trowel.

3 Set the first brick lengthwise on the mortar bed in one corner. Check it for level end to end and front to back. If it's out of level, tap the high corner with the end of the trowel handle. Spread a ⅝-inch-thick layer of mortar onto the end of a second brick. This is called "buttering" the brick. Bevel the edges inward with your trowel so the mortar mounds toward the center. Lay the brick into the mortar bed and at the same time press it against the first brick. The joint should compress and fill to ½ inch. Check and level this brick; then follow this procedure to lay two more bricks, checking for level faithfully and keeping the bricks within the chalk marks on the footing, as shown in figure 2.

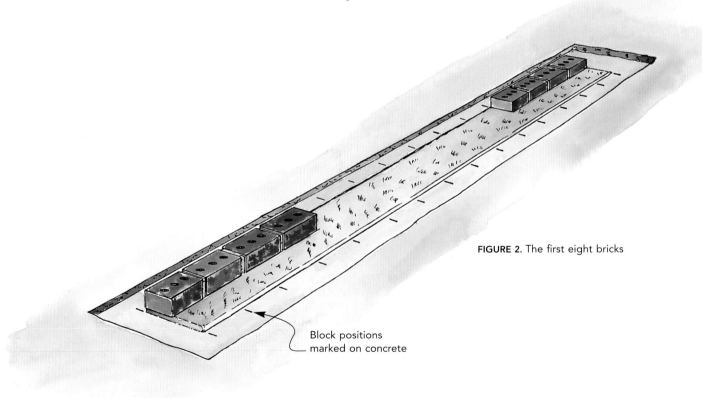

FIGURE 2. The first eight bricks

Block positions marked on concrete

4 Repeat step 3 on the opposite end of the wall. Attach the corner blocks with the mason's line to the top of both corner bricks, so the line is even with the tops of the bricks. Attach the line level and then adjust any bricks that aren't level. Once both ends of the wall are level, continue laying bricks toward the center of the wall from both ends, checking for level faithfully and keeping the bricks within the chalk marks on the footing. Lay the final brick in this row—called the "closure brick"—by buttering both ends and wiggling it into place. Check for level.

5 Complete the first course by laying a second row of bricks alongside the first. Check for level both along the length and across the two rows; then fill the joint between the rows with mortar. Use a pointing trowel to fill the exposed joints at each end if needed.

6 The rest of the wall is constructed by building up the ends first and then filling in the middle section, as shown in figure 3. Start building one end by spreading a second ⅝-inch layer of mortar on top of one end of the brick course you just completed. Lay the first brick of the second course across the two end bricks of the first course, and level it both ways, making a ½-inch joint. This crosswise brick will serve as a header that will make the second course of bricks overlap the first course by half, keeping the joints staggered so the wall will be stable.

7 Now add the next six bricks of the second course to the wall (two rows of three lengthwise bricks). On top of this, lay the start of the third course of bricks (two rows of three lengthwise bricks *without* a crosswise header). Then lay the start of the fourth course (one crosswise header and then two rows of two lengthwise bricks). Finish building up the wall end by laying the start of the fifth course (two rows of two lengthwise bricks). As you build, remember to check for level both along the length and across the width of the wall. Hold the carpenter's level against the end of the wall to check for plumb (as shown in figure 4), and use the story pole to check the height of each course as you build (see figure 3).

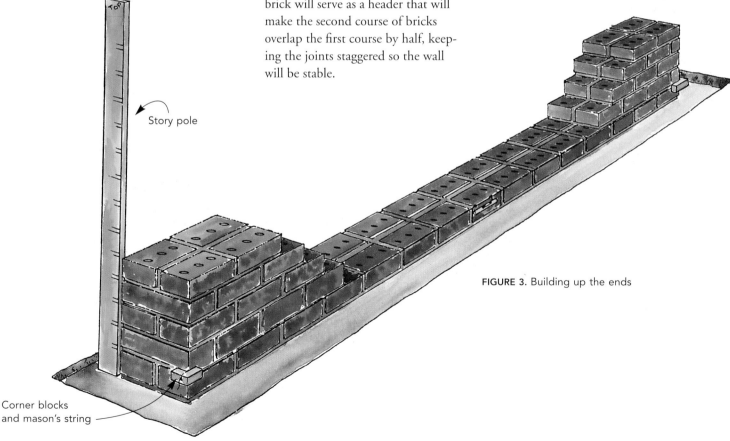

Story pole

Corner blocks and mason's string

FIGURE 3. Building up the ends

8 Repeat steps 6 and 7 to build up the other end of the wall. Once both ends of the wall are raised by five courses, scrape off any excess mortar with the edge of the trowel. A joint tool can be used to clean and smooth the joints.

9 Spread a bed of mortar, and lay the second brick course completely. Check for level individually and along the row as you work.

10 Spread a bed of mortar on top of the second course, and lay the third course. Continue laying courses, constantly checking for level and height with the story pole as you work. Build up end leads as you proceed with each course, remembering that every other course will begin and end with a crosswise brick.

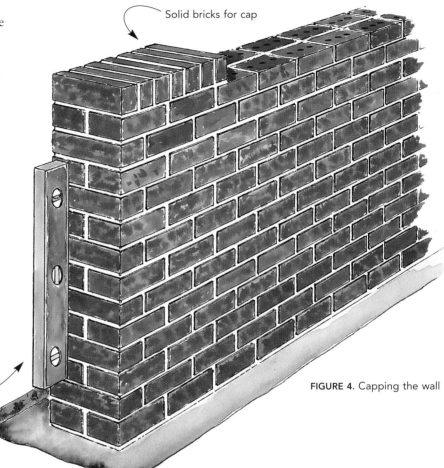

Solid bricks for cap

Carpenter's level

FIGURE 4. Capping the wall

11 Finish the top of the wall by capping it with a row of bricks laid on edge across the wall's width, as shown in figure 4. First lay a mortar bed along the top of the exposed course, then butter and lay the individual bricks on edge until the row is closed and complete. Make sure you use solid blocks on the ends and check for level both across and lengthwise.

12 Finish the joints by running the joint tool along vertical joints first, then along the horizontal joints. If there's a place where the joint isn't fully filled out, pack it with mortar using a pointing trowel; then smooth the joint with the tool.

project

Interlocking Concrete Block Retaining Wall

Tired of mowing that bank or watching your soil erode? The interlocking concrete block retaining wall systems available these days offer an easy-to-install solution for sloping ground. How the blocks actually connect differs somewhat from system to system, but the basic steps that follow apply to just about any retaining wall up to 4 feet tall. Give yourself plenty of time to complete this project; it's strenuous work that calls for lots of bending and heavy lifting.

MATERIALS

Compactible aggregate material (See Tip)

Sand

Crushed gravel

Interlocking concrete blocks

Cap blocks

Masonry adhesive

TIP

■ Compactible aggregate material is made up of various size gravel and sand that compacts into a solid base. Both the composition and the name of this material may differ, depending on where you live. It is *not* the same as the crushed gravel used to backfill behind the wall.

TOOLS AND SUPPLIES

Shovel

Hoe

Measuring tape

Mason's line

Line level

Tamper

Carpenter's level

Screed board (a 2 x 4, 28 inches long, would work well)

Broom

Stone hammer

Block chisel

Protective eyewear

Torpedo level

Circular saw with masonry blade (optional; see step 6)

Caulking gun

Pencil

INSTRUCTIONS

1 Excavate the slope where the wall will go, using the shovel or hoe. Retain this soil for later use. Measure and mark the lines for a trench— you'll need to leave 12 inches between the back edge of the trench and the soil bank (this is for the crushed gravel that will go between the wall and the bank. Dig the trench 18 to 24 inches wide and about 12 inches deep—or 8 inches deeper than the thickness of the blocks you're using— in order to accommodate a firm gravel base. Skim the bottom of the trench flat and level with a hoe, and check for true by stretching mason's line 6 inches above the ground end to end and hanging the line level from it.

2 Fill the trench with 4 to 6 inches of compactible aggregate material. Pack the material with the tamper, and use the carpenter's level to check for level as you work.

3 Add a 1-inch layer of sand on top of this base. Use the screed board to level the sand, checking your work once again with a carpenter's level. This tedious task is worth whatever time it takes—the structural integrity of your wall depends on its base being level and well-compacted.

4 Begin setting the base course of block. Space the blocks slightly apart for drainage, and check each one side to side and front to back as you align them, using a torpedo level. As you work along the wall's length, use the longer carpenter's level to check adjoining blocks (see figure 1). If a block is too low, add sand underneath to raise it; if it's too high, tap it down with a mallet to seat it. If the blocks you're working with have lips, dig out a groove in the sand to accommodate the lips for this first course. In some situations, you may need to remove

the lower lip with the stone hammer and the block chisel to allow the blocks to lie flat; be sure to wear protective eyewear when doing so.

5 Fill the space in front, behind, and between the blocks with the crushed gravel. Tamp it down, and sweep the upper surface of the blocks clean in preparation for the next course.

6 Set the second course of block on top of the first, with the center of each block bridging the joint of the blocks below, so all joints are staggered. Make certain the lip of each block hooks over and against the back of the blocks below it as shown in figure 2. If your particular block uses a different setback and locking method, follow the manufacturer's instructions. For exposed, flush-ended walls, you'll

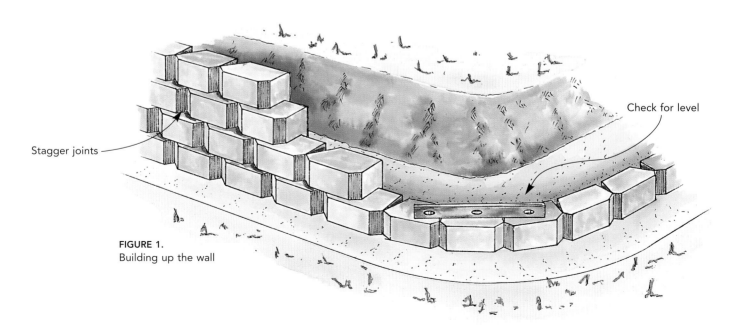

Stagger joints

Check for level

FIGURE 1.
Building up the wall

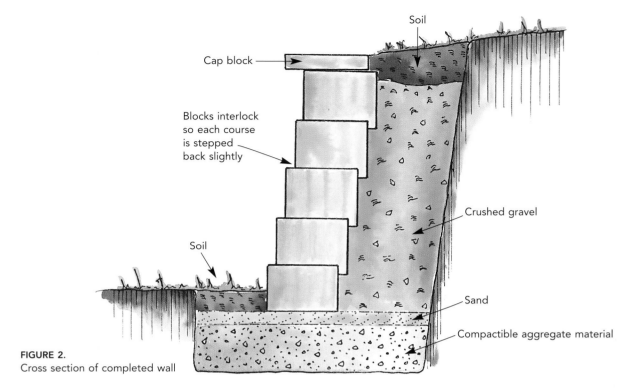

Soil

Cap block

Blocks interlock so each course is stepped back slightly

Crushed gravel

Soil

Sand

Compactible aggregate material

FIGURE 2.
Cross section of completed wall

have to begin and end each alternating course with a half-block. To split a block, score the top and bottom surface with the edge of the block chisel or the circular saw fitted with a masonry blade. Wet the score line and drive the chisel into the groove until it splits, as shown in figure 3. On walls where the ends will terminate into the slope, prepare a firm bed of foundation material adjacent to the last block, and place a full block over half of the block below so it rests firmly on both the lower block and the foundation material.

7 Continue laying the third and fourth courses of block, making sure the surface of the previous course is clean before installing the next. Backfill against the wall with several inches of gravel, and use soil from the excavation to fill towards the slope. Tamp all fill material after laying each course. At the final course of block, you can backfill with topsoil.

8 If the top of the wall will be exposed and not covered by plantings, you'll probably want to install cap block. This block is thinner than the structural block and is cemented in place using masonry adhesive and the caulking gun. It can be set flush with the face of the wall or allowed to overhang it. Dry-lay the cap block beforehand and mark its position in pencil. Then sweep the base block clean and cement the caps, using the marks as an alignment guide. Grade additional topsoil as needed to the surface of the cap, sloping it toward the face of the wall slightly so water will run over, and not pool behind, the structure.

FIGURE 3. Splitting a block

Dry-Stacked Stone Retaining Wall

When you need a wall to hold back a bank of soil, consider the simple beauty of a dry-stacked stone wall. Requiring neither mortar nor a concrete footer, a dry-stacked wall 2 feet or less in height can be constructed by just about any do-it-yourselfer. Just remember to pace yourself—this is a wall you'll probably want to build over the course of several weekends; otherwise, you may get some very sore muscles.

MATERIALS

Stones
Pea gravel (½-inch to
    ¾-inch stone)

TOOLS AND SUPPLIES

Shovel
Mattock (optional, see step 2)
Pick (optional, see step 2)
Wheelbarrow (for hauling stone)
1 piece of steel rebar, 3 feet long

TIPS

■ Heavy work gloves and sturdy boots are essential safety gear when working with stone.

■ These instructions are for dry-stacked walls 2 feet or less in height. Dry-stacked walls higher than this require larger stones and a more severe degree of batter (backwards slant); they are best left to experienced stone masons.

INSTRUCTIONS

1 The stones that will make up the top course of your wall are called *capstones*. These need to be fairly large and flat, so select some of these stones now and set them aside for later.

2 Use your shovel (and the mattock and pick, if necessary) to excavate the slope you will be retaining. The bank should angle back slightly from the bottom to the top (see figure 1). Use your mattock and pick to remove any rubble (small, irregularly shaped stones) and roots, so the face of the cut is smooth. Reserve the rubble stones and about one-fourth of this soil for later use.

3 Excavate the foundation for your wall by digging a 6-inch deep by 2-foot wide trench at the base of your cut bank. Fill this trench with pea gravel; then add a 2-inch-thick layer of pea gravel (that will rest above ground) on top of that.

4 The first course of the wall is made up of base stones. These should be the largest stones and should have at least one wide, flat surface (wedge the uneven face of any base stone into the pea gravel foundation). Lay out your base stones so that their front ends (at the front of the gravel foundation) are as close together as possible and their back ends are slanting down slightly. The stones at either end of your wall should reach all the way back to the cut bank, since these serve as cornerstones. If a cornerstone is short, find another stone that, when set close behind the first, will reach back to the bank and keep the gravel fill from washing out. The distance between the cut bank and the back of the rest of this first course should average about 1 inch.

5 Add any rubble stones you have available in the space between the base stones and the base. Then lock this first course in place by spreading pea gravel over the rubble and behind the base stones. Use the rebar to set

the gravel, especially between the gaps at the back edges of the stones. This step, while tedious, is essential for a strong, stable wall.

6 Brush off any gravel left on top of the base stones. Then lay out the next layer of stones, taking care to place each stone on top of a joint between two of the base stones. Doing so with each layer of the wall will help you avoid "running joints" (vertical gaps running down the wall), which weaken both the strength and the appearance of the wall. Remember, too, when positioning your stones, to maintain the wall's batter of 5 to 10°. Use small rocks as wedges or shims to keep stones level and stable.

7 The stablest walls will have a long "tie stone" running from the front of the wall all the way back to the bank every couple of courses and every 4 or 5 feet of wall length. If you can't find stones long enough to work as tie stones, place two stones close together to serve the same purpose.

8 Build up the wall by continuing to add courses of stone and carefully setting gravel backfill. Remember to constantly check that each course of stone is level from end to end and maintains the batter of 5 to 10°.

9 Lay out the final course of your wall with the capstones you set aside in step 1. Backfill with pea gravel again, but this time use the soil reserved in step 2 to cover the gravel.

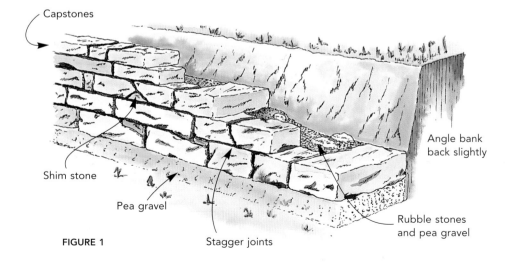

Capstones

Shim stone

Pea gravel

Stagger joints

Angle bank back slightly

Rubble stones and pea gravel

FIGURE 1

project

Landscape Timber Retaining Wall

A landscape-timber retaining wall can hold back sloping ground without a concrete footing or mortared joints. The straightforward construction method and relatively inexpensive materials make this wall a favorite with do-it-yourselfers. Just make sure your bank can be retained by a wall 3 feet or lower in height. Taller walls call for more structural support, and walls higher than 4 feet usually must be designed by an engineer.

MATERIALS

Compactible aggregate material
    (see Tips)

Pressure-treated landscape timbers
    (see Tips)

½-inch reinforcing bar,
    36 inches long

12-inch galvanized spikes

Perforated drainpipe

Crushed gravel

TOOLS AND SUPPLIES

Shovel

Measuring tape

Stakes

Mason's line

Tamper

Carpenter's level

Sledgehammer

Drill

⅝-inch spade bit

¼- and 1-inch spade bits
    (optional, see steps 4 and 6)

Chainsaw (optional, see step 3)

Circular saw with a framing blade
    (optional, see step 3)

Handsaw (optional, see step 3)

Safety gear (see Tips)

TIPS

■ Pressure-treated 5 x 6 timbers in 8-foot lengths are a good choice for this project. They're less expensive than larger beams, and if you stack them so they're 6 inches high, calculations will be simple.

■ Because pressure-treated wood contains the preservative CCA (chromated copper arsenate), wear work gloves when handling the timbers, and add a dust mask and protective eyewear when cutting them.

■ Compactible aggregate material is made up of various size gravel and sand that compacts into a solid base. Both the composition and the name of this material may differ, depending on where you live. It's not the same as the crushed gravel used to backfill behind the wall.

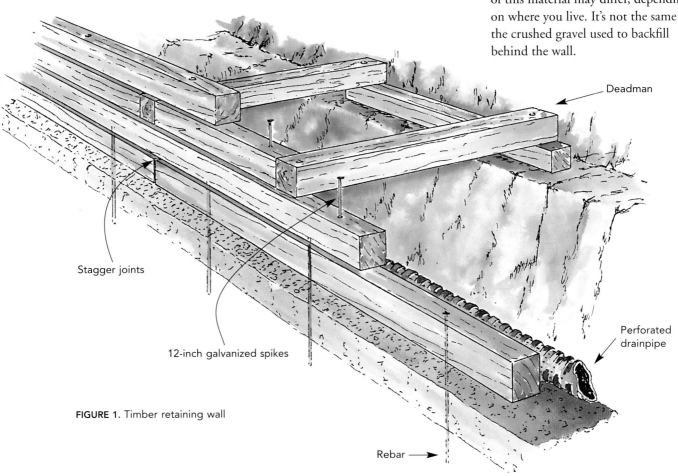

Stagger joints

12-inch galvanized spikes

Deadman

Perforated drainpipe

Rebar

FIGURE 1. Timber retaining wall

INSTRUCTIONS

1 Excavate and level the portion of the slope where the wall will go. Set this soil aside for use in later steps. If the wall will be more than two or three courses high, you'll need a 12-inch-wide trench to bed the first course of timbers. Lay out the trench with stakes and the mason's line. Dig to a depth of 6 inches in firm soil. (In loose or sandy soil—or soils subject to frost heave—dig a 12-inch-deep trench.) Spread a 6-inch layer of compactible aggregate material in it. Tamp the material flat, and check it with the carpenter's level.

2 Set the first course of timbers and level them with the sledgehammer. Anchor these foundation timbers by first boring ⅝-inch holes through each timber, 16 inches from the ends, and one in the center, as shown in figure 1. Then drive 36-inch lengths of ½-inch reinforcing bar, "rebar," through the holes and into the ground until they're flush with the top of the wood. To further stabilize these bottom timbers, pack some of the soil removed from the trench against the front face of the timbers to create a slight slope away from the retaining wall.

3 Lay up the second course so that each timber is set over the joint between two timbers on the course below, as shown in figure 1. This will avoid "running joints" that weaken the wall's structure. Set this and all following courses ¾ inch back from the one below it, unless you're retaining only 12 inches or less of soil. (This setback allows the wall to lean back into the slope for greater strength.) Cut the timbers to the correct length with a chainsaw if one is available. Otherwise, use a framing blade in a circular saw, and rotate the timber so you can cut in on all four sides to the blade's maximum 2⅜-inch depth. The cut will then need to be completed with a handsaw.

4 As you set each timber in place, nail it to the course below with 12-inch galvanized spikes, starting at about 8 inches from each end and then at 16-inch intervals in between. If you have trouble driving the spikes with the sledgehammer, predrill the top-course holes with a ¼-inch spade bit.

5 Starting at the second or third course, you'll need to install anchors or "deadmen" that run perpendicularly to stabilize the wall against the pressure of the soil being retained. (This is especially important for walls taller than 3 feet.) For the low wall in the photograph on page 45, deadmen were set two at a time, spaced 4 feet apart in the front and attached in the back by a 5-foot-long timber. Higher walls will need deadmen installed at every third or fourth course.

6 Once you've set a few courses, you will need to install perforated drainpipe to carry away excess water. Use your level to check the slope—it should be about ¼ inch for every foot of pipe run, and graded toward an opening you've planned. You can cut an exit hole through the joint of two courses with a chainsaw if you need to exit through an end wall. Lay the pipe about 6 inches behind the wall, and cover it with the crushed gravel as you work upward. Lower walls that will not have to deal with much water can be drained by drilling 1-inch weep holes every 4 feet through the timbers just above the base course, or about 12 inches above the ground.

7 Backfill the area behind the wall and drainpipe with soil removed from the excavation. Compact the earth with a tamper and continue to fill the area above the drainpipe with gravel as you work. When the last two courses are completed, backfill with topsoil, graded to rise just above the top timbers so any runoff will spill over the wall and not pool behind it.

Fences

chapter

3

IF YOU'RE THE IMPATIENT TYPE, a fence may well be the border for you. Walls go up and hedges *grow* up slower than fences. No matter what your site conditions or the functions desired, chances are good a fence exists that will work for you. And it will do that work while taking up very little of your ground space— a real bonus in small yards.

Fences usually cost less than a wall but more than a hedge of the same size. While the average fence requires more maintenance than the typical wall, the amount of upkeep required by a specific fence varies widely, depending on the materials and finish used. All this goes a long way toward explaining why fences are the most popular of garden borders. But the number one reason is probably the fact that there are so many different styles and variations of fencing from which to choose. With the information from the first chapter in mind, let the guide that follows help you narrow your search for the perfect border.

The cheerful picket fence is a staple of backyards everywhere.

Picket

Picket fences are friendly. Typically 3 to 4 feet high, they set a boundary without discouraging neighborly chats, the passing of borrowed cups of sugar, or peeks to check whose tomatoes are ripening first. We tend to think of picket fences as being as American as apple pie, but in fact, they were used in China as early as the eighth century A.D. and were also common in medieval gardens.

Most picket fences consist of a framework of 4 x 4 posts and 2 x 4 rails with an infill of pickets made from 1 x 3s or 1 x 4s. Preassembled 8-foot sections of fence are available—these usually come with pointed or square picket tops. If you install individual pickets, you can cut the tops to practically any style and even vary the lengths of the pickets so each bay of the completed fence curves.

This style of fence works well if your priorities are establishing a visual boundary, directing human traffic, or creating a backdrop for plants.

Pointed pickets discourage climbing (in either direction), but the fences are usually too short to keep determined intruders out or climbing pets in. In keeping with its friendly attitude, a picket fence offers little in the way of privacy. Relatively inexpensive to build, picket fences are usually painted or stained, so they will require regular maintenance (unless you are cunning enough to convince a friend that the privilege can be his in exchange for a dead rat on a string).

Board

This fence means business. It's about as close to a wall as a fence can get. At the same time, this no-nonsense boundary offers countless design variations. In fact, few fences have as many design options as the board fence. The size of the infill can vary from fence to fence (or even on the same fence), the boards can abut, have gaps in between, overlap, or—in the case of a shadow fence—be spaced on both sides of a central nailer to provide both privacy and airflow.

Usually, a board fence frame consists of 4 x 4 posts with two or three 2 x 4 horizontal rails attached. The infill is typically vertical boards that can be as narrow as 1 x 3s or as wide as 1 x 12s (boards that are 6 to 8 inches wide are ideal—narrower lumber is not economical, and very wide boards are more apt to warp or crack). This type of fence is fairly difficult (and therefore also fairly expensive) to build.

Consider a board fence if you need privacy, shade, security, or a reduction in noise. (Be careful, though: set in the path of prevailing winds, a solid board fence can cause downdrafts.) The sunny side of a board fence can provide a warm spot to grow tender plants. Plants, especially climbers, will also help soften the sometimes stark appearance of a newly installed board fence. Maintenance needs will vary, depending on whether the fence is painted, stained, or—if made from naturally rot-resistant or pressure-treated wood—left to weather naturally.

What might have been a boring board fence is made elegant by the simple curves at its top.

Stakes and Palings

Descending from the fortress-like palisades that surrounded early settlements, fences made from stakes and palings still have a somewhat imposing air about them. The rough, unsawn texture of the wood gives these fences a rustic appearance that fits in well with rural settings or informal gardens.

The fences are made by attaching split stakes or saplings with sharp, pointed tops to a framework of 4 x 4 posts and 2 x 4 rails. Construction is relatively simple, but the amount of infill required makes the work time-consuming and the cost high (unless you have a free supply of saplings).

Because of their pointed tops and close-set infill, these fences excel at providing both security and privacy. They're effective at delineating boundaries and tempering the environment (although downdrafts can occur if the infill is spaced too tightly). Left to weather naturally, palings from rot-resistant or pressure-treated wood should require little maintenance. If a stake fence is stained, maintenance needs will increase.

This rustic fence would look out of place in many settings but fits in well with this rural home.

Lattice's open construction makes it perfect for roses and other plants prone to fungal diseases.

Lattice

Lattice fencing has been a favorite with gardeners for centuries. Its crisscross design allows for lovely plays of light and seems to beg for the companionship of a climbing rose or clematis. Despite the open, airy effect of lattice, it can—depending on the closeness of the slats—offer a surprising degree of privacy, and it casts an acceptable amount of shade for most gardens. Circular (or other shaped) windows can be cut into lattice fencing to open up attractive views within or beyond the garden. The open nature of lattice helps it to diffuse winds. If the structure is easily climbed, it won't make effective security fencing (although especially thorny roses might help matters here).

You can purchase lattice in prefabricated 4 x 8-foot panels of cedar or treated wood. Most lattice fences consist of a frame of posts and upper and lower rails. The lattice panels are held in place with 1 x 1 strips (nailers) on either side of the posts. The cap rail across the top is typically straight, but fences of this type with scalloped tops are stunning. Lattice fencing is fairly easy and quick to install, so it is relatively inexpensive. The heavier (and more costly) grade of lattice will save you money in the long run. Make sure the staples holding the slats together are galvanized. Maintenance needs will depend on whether the fence is painted or stained or—if built from rot-resistant or pressure-treated wood—left to weather naturally.

This recently installed galvanized steel fence could pass itself off as a fine antique.

Ornamental Metal

A favorite of the Victorians, ornamental iron fences were so common in Europe, they were melted down and turned into weapons during World War II. Now craftspeople with the ability to hammer heated iron into the twists and arabesques of an ornamental fence are hard to find. Most of us must be content with the prefabricated sections of tubular steel or aluminum available at home centers.

Though metal fences are most commonly found in cityscapes, wrought iron looks spectacular with clematis or roses climbing up and through its intricate rails. The delicate patterns of light and shade cast by such a fence are also a charming addition to most gardens. The more ornamental of these fences have a formal appearance that complements houses with traditional architecture, while the sleeker, more modern style of metal fence works best with contemporary homes.

To provide security, a metal fence must be tall with narrow spaces between the infill, and preferably spiked tops. These characteristics, combined with a low clearance at the bottom, will also give you a fence that can keep pets and children contained.

Low ornamental metal fences are usually found at the front of the yard, where they serve mainly as psychological barriers. They don't provide much in the way of privacy; but let's face it, if you can afford to surround your yard with an iron fence, you probably want to show off the house and yard the fence encloses. Maintenance will depend in a large part on the quality of the fence. Check when purchasing one or having one installed for warranties against rust and corrosion.

Basket Weave

These handsome fences, made from woven slats of thin lumber, should appeal to the crafter who likes to work on a really large scale! (Those less ambitious can purchase prewoven panels to construct the fence.) Weaving the slats is actually easier than you may think, but it does take time. The cost of the materials for the slats or for the prewoven panels is generally moderate.

Effective at providing privacy while allowing air circulation, a basket weave fence is also good for delineating boundaries and tempering the environment. Its effectiveness as a security fence depends on the strength of its wood and the ease with which its framework can be climbed. Such fences look quite striking when stained, but, with all those woven surfaces, that can be a daunting task. If low maintenance is a priority, build yours from rot-resistant or pressure-treated wood and leave it to weather naturally.

This striking basket weave fence makes the grade, while separating a backyard from an alley.

Decorative details can help break the monotony of a panel fence.

Panel

The effect of a panel fence is similar to that of an interior house wall. Panel fences are usually constructed with plywood as the infill, but hardboard, plastic, fiberglass, and even glass itself are also options. These tend to be contemporary-looking fences; they don't fit in well with every type of setting. The solid face of this kind of fence will provide a backdrop for plants, but it can feel overwhelming in too small a space.

Panel fences usually go up quickly; their cost will depend on the materials used as infill. Solid ones are excellent at providing privacy and can keep intruders out and pets and children in if their framework is not easily climbed. A panel fence will provide a microclimate for plants, but openings must be designed into the structure to avoid downdrafts in windy sites. The maintenance needs of a panel fence will depend on the material it's built from, but since these fences are usually painted or stained, they need continual upkeep.

Post-and-Rail and Post-and-Board

These are rural fences. They're descendants of the rustic stacked-rail worm fences that once zigzagged their way across the American landscape (and which George Washington once declared "expensive and wasteful of lumber"). The pared-down version in use today requires considerably less lumber than most fences and is often used to enclose a large area while still maintaining a view.

These fences can be rustic (as in the case of split-rail fencing) or rather stately (as with the white post-and-board fences surrounding many horse farms). Typically, such fences consist of mortised posts fitted with two to four tenoned rails or dadoed posts with boards. The cost will depend on the type and amount of wood used.

Traditionally used to keep livestock contained, these fences are also effective at delineating boundaries, directing foot traffic, and providing a place for roses to ramble. They don't provide security or privacy, nor do they temper the environment (except for blocking drifting snow). If constructed from rot-resistant or pressure-treated wood and left to weather naturally, these fences will require little in the way of maintenance. Ones that are painted or stained will require regular upkeep.

This three-rail fence establishes a clear border without detracting from the beauty of the landscape.

Bamboo

Bamboo is actually a woody grass with hollow, upright stems. According to a Taoist belief, each individual section of the plant's stem represents a step along the path to enlightenment. Traditionally found in the Far East, bamboo fences bring an exotic touch to the garden. They do, however, look out of place in many settings. A bamboo fence that might be stunning in front of a contemporary home on the rugged California coast would look silly in the front yard of a New England Colonial. On the other hand, a bamboo fence is the perfect border for a Japanese-style garden or a backyard koi pond.

Borders made from bamboo can be open or closed, simple or elaborate, depending on their design. Since bamboo usually must be purchased through mail order and shipped, bamboo fences are costly. A less expensive option is to purchase rolls of wire-bound bamboo (which can be found at many home improvement centers) and use them to erect a temporary screen. How long a bamboo fence will last in your area depends on the climate (immature or improperly cured bamboo will decay quickly in a humid environment) and the construction of the fence (treated posts or galvanized steel pipe should be used for the parts of the fence that go into the ground). The warm honey color of bamboo will weather to gray eventually unless you apply an occasional coat of wax or the waterproofing sealers used on decks.

Because bamboo fences come in so many styles, it should be possible (although not always practical) to find one to meet your needs. The most common function of a bamboo fence is as a divider or screen within the garden.

Bamboo's flexibility allows for the sinuous curves and light, airy design of this elegant handcrafted fence.

Chain link disguised with a closely planted hedge helps keep this pool safe and secure.

Chain Link

No one installs a chain-link fence for decorative purposes—this is always a fence with a job to do. We may be use to thinking of chain link as fit only for jobs such as keeping snarling dogs confined to junkyards, but the right chain link fence in the right place can be both hardworking and, well, if not exactly attractive, at least unobtrusive.

The fence consists of wire mesh attached to straining wires held taut by posts. The wire should be galvanized or coated with colored plastic. Chain-link fences that are coated with black plastic will blend most readily into the landscape. Growing an evergreen hedge against green chain link will make the fence less obtrusive.

Chain link is one of the less-expensive fencing options and is fairly easy to install once you get the hang of it. Excellent at providing security, chain-link fences offer little in the way of privacy unless they are heavily planted or special inserts are installed. They give climbing plants a leg up but offer little in the way of a micro-climate except for blocking drifting snow and serving as a windbreak if densely planted. A well-constructed chain-link fence should need little in the way of maintenance.

Wattle

This attractive fence, evocative of the English countryside, derives much of its charm from its rustic simplicity. Consisting of little more than a row of posts driven into the ground and then woven with thin, flexible saplings, this fence has been used since ancient times. The wattle fence is not a long-lasting structure; when used to enclose fields in Europe, it also provided a perch for birds, which then excreted seeds such as bramble and hawthorn. The seeds germinated to become mixed hedges that grew up as the wattle slowly deteriorated. American colonists put wattle fences up as temporary borders until more substantial ones could be erected.

Wattle fencing is usually purchased as individual screens, called hurdles, and will be expensive unless you happen to live close to a hurdle-maker. If you can gather long whips of willow, hazel, bamboo, hickory (or just about any flexible green wood) locally, consider weaving your own hurdles. Much of the character of these handmade fences comes from their imperfections—they're a good choice for those intimidated by power tools or frustrated by the precise leveling and exact measurements most fences call for. Once erected, wattles will require little in the way of maintenance, but they also won't last longer than five to ten years.

Because of this, wattles are most often used as internal boundaries in a garden, providing a screen to shade a patio or to hide the compost pile. They look lovely with flowers such as morning glories or nasturtiums climbing up them, and they are equally at home in the vegetable garden, covered with snow peas or cherry tomatoes.

This low wattle border is being used as a rustic edging beside a walkway.

Woven Willow

Make a simple but enchanting fence by inserting long willow sticks into the ground at opposite angles and then weaving them together. The willow will often take root and become a leafy living border. Perfect beside a kitchen garden, the fence will not only mark a boundary, but it will also provide a fair amount of privacy (especially when it is in leaf), wind protection, and shade.

Willow whips can be purchased from suppliers, but in many places it's possible to gather your own from riverbanks and roadsides. (Always ask permission before gathering from private property.) Constructing the fence is a simple if fairly time-consuming task (instructions are provided on page 76). If you're interested in growing a woven willow fence, plan ahead—willow is most likely to take root (and is also easiest to weave) if you make the fence in early spring, when the plants are still dormant.

This delightfully planted willow fence provides a charming screen that changes with the seasons.

Setting Fence Posts

BOTH THE APPEARANCE AND THE DURABILITY of your fence depend on properly set posts. Time spent to do this task right will be time saved on maintenance and repairs for years to come. Prior to digging, make certain there are no buried utility cables, gas, or water lines in the immediate vicinity of your work. Usually, the local utility companies will check and flag the location of underground services at no charge. You can also hire a company that specializes in locating underground utilities (listed in your phone book's business section under "Utilities Underground Cable, Pipe & Wire Locating Service"). Also, check with your local building department to determine the frost depth in your area and whether frost heave is a concern. In many northern climates, moist, fine-grained soils are subject to winter freezing and thawing cycles, which cause the earth to shift and dislocate even firmly set fence posts. Where frost heave is a problem, the holes must be dug below the frost line and the posts set in a suitable drainage medium.

INSTRUCTIONS

1 Use a posthole digger to excavate a hole about 4 inches deeper than the depth you plan to set the post. Generally, posts should be set at a minimum of 24 inches, or with at least one-third of their total length in the ground. Gate posts and end and corner posts, which support greater weight, should meet or exceed the one-third rule if possible. Keep the hole width as narrow as possible—about twice the diameter of the post you are planting—unless you intend to use stabilizing cleats or concrete fill (see step 4), in which case you can make the hole three times the thickness of the post.

2 Shovel about 4 inches of ¾-inch gravel into the bottom of the hole and tamp it firmly with a piece of 2 x 4. Reset any layout lines you're using to mark the face of the post instead of its center.

3 If you are setting posts that already have mortises or dadoes cut into them, they'll need to be set to exact height. This is made easier by temporarily attaching cleats (usually lengths of 1 x 4) to the posts that will hold the posts in the holes at the proper height (see figure 1). First determine how much of the post you want to have aboveground; then measure down that distance from the top of each post. Use No. 8 x 1½ decking screws to attach cleats to the post at that point.

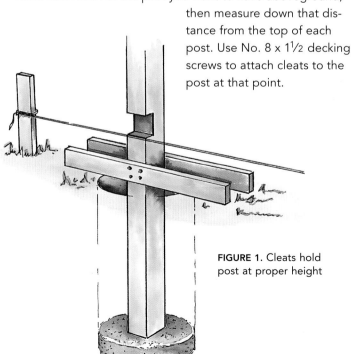

FIGURE 1. Cleats hold post at proper height

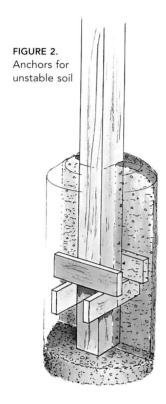

FIGURE 2.
Anchors for unstable soil

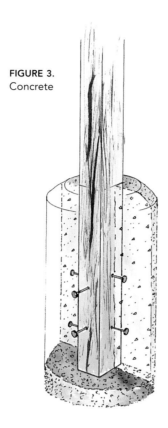

FIGURE 3.
Concrete

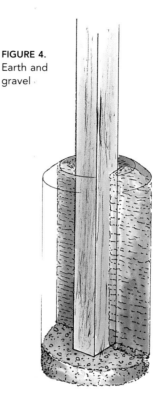

FIGURE 4.
Earth and gravel

4 In loose, sandy, or unstable soil, anchors can be used to keep posts firmly in the ground (see figure 2). These are often pressure-treated 1 x 4 strips cut in length to about two and a half times the thickness of the post and nailed to its sides about two-thirds into the depth of the hole. If you're using concrete fill, you can sink six or eight 16-penny galvanized nails into the post at that point (see figure 3).

5 Replace the post in the holes against the layout line, and use a level to determine plumb in both directions. In most soils you can now fill the hole with an earth and gravel mix (see figure 4), tamping with a length of 2 x 4 as you go until you reach the surface. If you plan to use concrete fill, mix all materials dry (even bagged premix) in a wheelbarrow, then add water to make a thick slurry. Shovel the concrete into the hole and tamp it with a 2 x 4 to remove air bubbles. You can either fill the hole completely with concrete, or you can backfill with more gravel to within 4 inches of the surface, tamp, and pour a concrete cap at the top. Trowel the cap downward from the post to shed water.

6 Concrete-bedded posts must be braced for a period of at least 24 hours. Drive a wooden stake about 2 feet from the post on two adjacent sides. Nail a 2 x 4 between each of the stakes and the top of the post, checking for plumb before securing each one. As a general rule, end posts should be set first, then line posts set against the layout lines established between the posts. Fence rails and infill are installed after the posts are set. For mortised or precut fencing, the posts are set as each successive section is completed. Remove the stakes and bracing after the posts are set.

Building Fences on Slopes

Building a fence on sloped ground is a difficult but not insurmountable challenge. Fences can transcend sloped terrain in two ways. Either they can be stepped—each section of fence set at equal intervals to match the rise of the slope, akin to a set of stairs (see figure 2)—or they can be contoured, in which the rails run parallel with the slope, and the fence follows the contour of the ground (see figure 3, page 66).

To plot a fence that will be built on a slope, you'll need 100 feet of mason's line, a steel tape measure, a torpedo level and a line level, a plumb bob, masking tape or ribbon, nails, and pieces of cloth. You'll also need a hefty hammer and two wooden stakes (one needs only be 1 foot tall, the other must be tall enough to extend at least 1 foot above the top of the slope when inserted into the ground at the downhill end of the fenceline—see figure 1).

To lay out a stepped fence, start at the beginning point uphill, drive the first stake firmly into the ground, and check it for two-way plumb (sideways and forward-and-back) with the torpedo level. This stake does not need to be particularly tall, but it does have to be stable. Then place the taller stake at the end point downhill and drive it into the ground, plumbed both ways as before.

Tie one end of the mason's line to the first stake and stretch the line to the other stake. Hang the line level on the line at the midpoint, and tie the line to the second stake at the point that it is level.

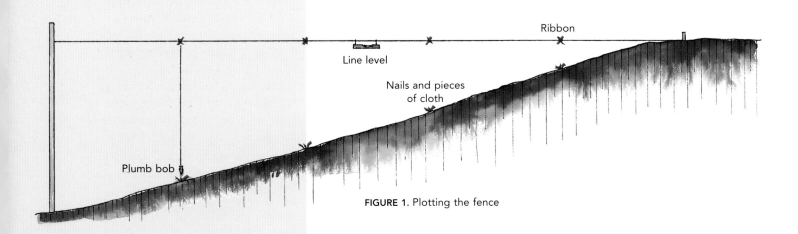

Ribbon

Line level

Nails and pieces
of cloth

Plumb bob

FIGURE 1. Plotting the fence

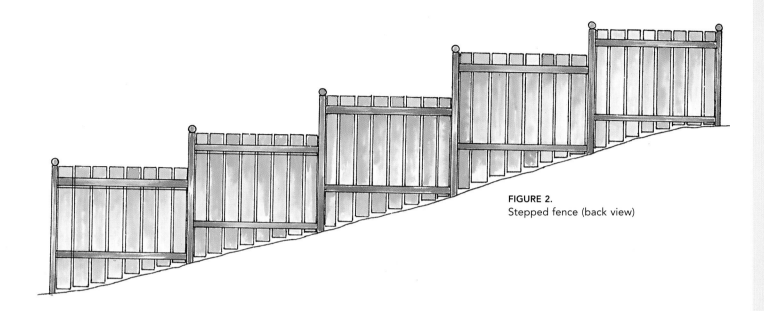

FIGURE 2.
Stepped fence (back view)

If the slope is fairly gradual, your line will cover some distance before the downhill stake becomes too short to hold the string at level. On a steep slope, the line may only extend 10 or 12 feet before staking. If your intended fence or wall goes beyond the point of the second stake, you'll need to drive a third stake in line downhill from that, and tie another length of mason's line from the base of the second stake to the top of the third stake so it is level. A fourth or fifth stake might also be required, depending on the topography of your site.

With that done, you can mark the locations for each fence post. Measure along the leveled line(s) and divide the total distance by the length you've planned for each fence section. The sections should be kept at some standard—perhaps 4, 6, or 8 feet—to make best use of precut lumber sizes. So, for example, if your total run is 36 feet and you've planned 6-foot sections, you can accommodate six sections within your fence run. Any remainder can be dropped, or if needed, the line extended to include the additional section. Use tape or ribbon to mark the locations along the level line where each fence post will fall.

These points can then be used as references to transfer the marked locations to the ground. Hang your plumb bob alongside each ribbon without distorting the line, and mark the ground at the pendulum point with nails and pieces of cloth, as shown in figure 1.

To determine the size of each step in the fence, you'll have to figure the overall rise, or height, of the slope. On a single-line layout, this is simply a matter of measuring the distance from the ground to the string at the downhill stake. On multiple-line layouts, that measurement must be taken at each successive downhill stake, and the results added together.

Since the most attractive stepped fences maintain the same step height between sections, you'll want to divide the total rise by the number of sections to arrive at a consistent dimension for each step. So, if the rise is 60 inches and you are planning six equal sections, there will be a 10-inch step between each section of fence. These can be measured from the top of each line post and marked in pencil for later reference when you are setting the posts.

Plotting a contoured fence is even simpler than laying out a stepped structure. Begin by driving a long stake into the starting point at the high end of the slope. Then drive and plumb a second stake into the ground at the end point downhill. Run mason's line between the two stakes, tying it the same distance from the ground at both ends. The line should clear any obstructions or abrupt changes in terrain. If it does-n't, you may have to drive additional stakes between the two points to keep the line clear.

Once the line is strung, begin at the uphill stake and measure down along the line, marking the locations of each fence post with tape to correspond with the length you've chosen for each fence section. Then use a plumb bob, as described before, to transfer those post locations to the ground, where they should be marked with flagged nails.

When it comes time to install the posts for a contoured fence, each one is set to exactly the same height above the ground, so that the fence line follows the terrain's natural contour (see figure 3). This can be accomplished by either backfilling the holes and tamping the posts as needed to achieve the precise height required, or simply setting the posts to "run wild" in length, and trimming their tops accordingly once they're in place. The rail locations are then marked at a consistent height along the posts, measured at an appropriate distance above the ground.

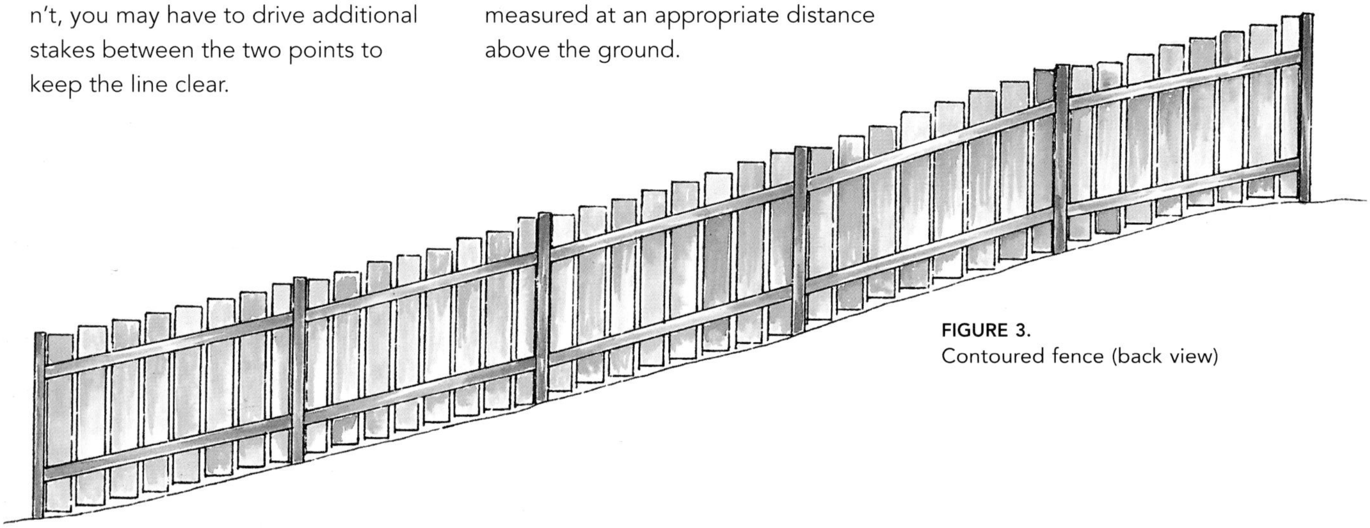

FIGURE 3.
Contoured fence (back view)

Stick Fence

his rustic fence will surround your garden with simple charm, while offering a place for climbers to run riot. Essentially a homespun version of the picket fence, this unpretentious border provides the perfect backdrop for an informal garden. Gathering the fence's infill will require some stick-to-it-tiveness, so tackle this project a little at a time, as befits its laid-back style.

TIPS

■ Green hardwood saplings will make the best sticks for this fence. If you don't have a source on your property, clean up (always with permission) behind power companies, road construction crews, or new building projects. Use pruners or loppers to remove any branches from the sticks.

■ Use only pressure-treated lumber or naturally decay-resistant wood (such as cedar, redwood, locust, osage orange, or cypress) for the posts and rails. Because pressure-treated wood contains the preservative CCA (chromated copper arsenate), wear work gloves when handling it, and add a dust mask and protective eyewear when cutting it.

■ If you're enclosing a garden and want to keep animals out, attach hardware cloth from the lower rail down to the ground before attaching the stick pickets.

MATERIALS

Green hardwood saplings (see Tips)

4 x 4 fence posts, 6- or 8-feet tall

2 x 4 rails, 6- or 8-feet long

Sticks (see Tips)

Hammer

Masking tape or ribbon

Strips of cloth

¾-inch gravel

No. 8 x 3-inch weatherized deck screws

2-inch galvanized finishing nails

TOOLS AND SUPPLIES

Tape measure

1 x 2 stakes, 12-inches tall

Mason's line

Line level

Plumb bob

Posthole digger

Carpenter's level

Hammer

Loppers

THE FOLLOWING MATERIALS ARE NECESSARY IF SETTING POSTS IN CONCRETE:

Concrete

Wheelbarrow

Shovel

Water

16d galvanized nails

Trowel

INSTRUCTIONS

1 Lay out your fence by measuring a distance along your intended line and driving 1 x 2 stakes into the ground to indicate the location of your two end posts. It will simplify matters later if you make this distance a multiple of your rail length, such as 6 or 8 feet. Then drive two more stakes into the ground, each about 2 feet back from an end-post stake. Stretch mason's line between the two outermost stakes with a line level attached at the midpoint. Make sure the line is taut and level.

2 Measure along the string line between the end-post stakes and divide the total distance by the length of your rails. For instance, if your total run is 36 feet and you're using 6-foot rails, you can fit six sections within the run, and you'll need seven postholes. Use masking tape or ribbon to mark the locations along the string line where each post will fall. Then hang a plumb bob alongside each ribbon and mark that point on the ground with a nail and a strip of cloth. Use the posthole digger to excavate the individual postholes to a depth of 3 feet, centered at the marked points.

3 Set the end posts in place, following the procedure described in Setting Fence Posts, on page 62. Use the carpenter's level to plumb the end posts; then backfill the holes.

4 Reset the mason's line against the end posts once they're fixed in place. Using this string line, set the line posts in place at the proper height, then plumb in both directions and backfill.

5 Using the top of one end post as a reference, measure down to the point where the upper edge of the top rail will go and mark it. Then measure down to the top of the planned lower rail, and make a mark for it. Repeat for all the posts.

6 Measure the center-to-center distance between each post as a double check prior to cutting the rails. Then trim the rails to the proper length. Each rail should butt the one next to it at the midpoint of the post. If that's not the case, minor adjustments can be made by trimming the rails slightly—but remember that they must abut at a post for support. Use the marks made in step 5 to position the rails and then fasten them to the outside of the posts with No. 8 x 3-inch weatherized deck screws.

7 Use 2-inch galvanized finishing nails, driven in at an angle, to attach the sticks to the outside of the rails (positioning the sticks about 4 inches apart will give you a pleasing degree of density). The sticks should touch the ground and extend a bit higher than the desired final fence height.

8 Trim the tops of the sticks with sharp loppers, either straight across or in a pattern of your choice. The bottoms of the fence should be trimmed just above the ground.

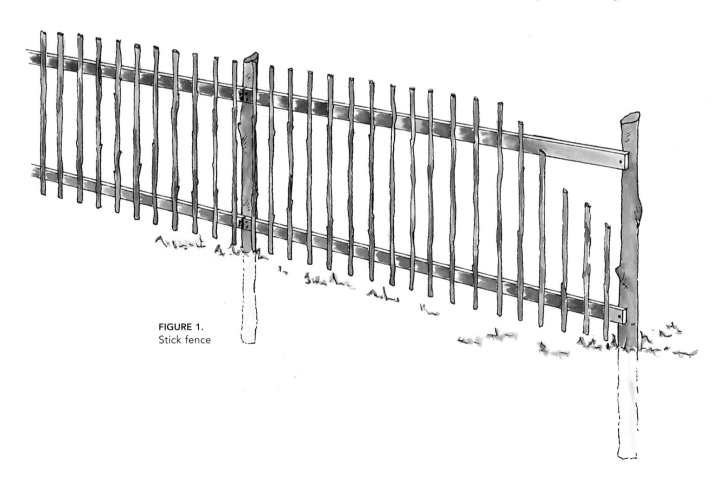

FIGURE 1.
Stick fence

project

Post-and-Rail Fence

MATERIALS

Premortised and tenoned posts and rails (rails are usually 6 or 8 feet long)

1 x 2 stakes, 12 inches long

Masking tape or ribbon

Strips of cloth

¾-inch gravel

TOOLS AND SUPPLIES

Tape measure

Mason's line

Line level

Plumb bob

Posthole digger

Carpenter's level

THE FOLLOWING MATERIALS ARE NECESSARY IF SETTING POSTS IN CONCRETE:

Concrete

Wheelbarrow

Shovel

Water

16d galvanized nails

Trowel

TIP

■ Mowing and weeding around the posts of this kind of fence can be difficult. If your fence spans a patch of lawn, lay landscape fabric around the base of newly set posts, or consider planting a low-maintenance groundcover at the base of each post.

Here's a fence that will look at home in front of most suburban ranch houses. The style of the fence will vary somewhat depending on whether the rails are split, square, or round. The wood for post-and-rail fences can be found at most large home centers and lumberyards. Because the fence kits are sold with the posts already mortised and tenons precut into the rails, assembly is a snap.

INSTRUCTIONS

1 Lay out your fence by measuring a distance along your intended line and driving 1 x 2 stakes into the ground to indicate the location of your two end posts. Make this distance between the end posts a multiple of your rail length, usually 6 or 8 feet. Then drive two more stakes into the ground, each about 2 feet back from an end-post stake. Stretch mason's line between the two outermost stakes with a line level attached at the midpoint. Make sure the line is taut and level.

2 Measure along the string line between the two end-post stakes and divide the total distance by your rail length. So, if your total run is 36 feet and your rails are 6 feet long, you can fit six sections within the run, and you'll need seven postholes. Use tape or ribbon to mark the locations along the string line where each post will fall. Then hang a plumb bob alongside each ribbon and mark that point on the ground with a nail and a strip of cloth.

3 Follow the steps in Setting Fence Posts, page 62, to set the first post only. Because the posts are already mortised, they must be set to an exact height; the instructions for using cleats to do so can also be found on page 62. Remember, too, that with this type of fence, the posts must be set one at a time, as each section of the fence is assembled.

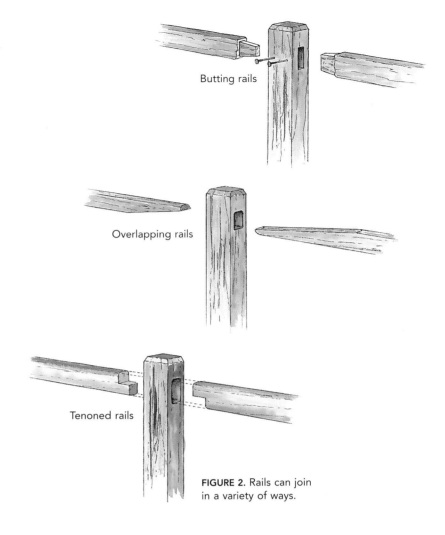

Butting rails

Overlapping rails

Tenoned rails

FIGURE 2. Rails can join in a variety of ways.

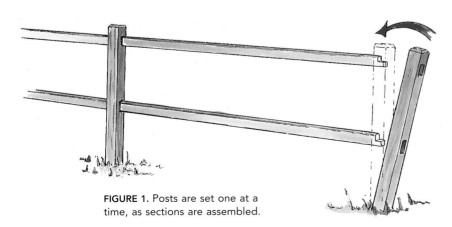

FIGURE 1. Posts are set one at a time, as sections are assembled.

4 Once the first post has been set, position the second post into its hole. Insert the rails into the first post, then connect the second post to the rails, as shown in figure 1.

5 Use the carpenter's level to make sure the second post is plumb and the rails are level. Then you can set the second post permanently.

6 Repeat steps 4 and 5 until the fence is completed.

project

Picket Fence

his is the friendly fence. Build one, and your neighbors are apt to stop and chat when they pass by. Large home centers now offer prefabricated panels of picket fencing that go up quickly, but if you build your picket fence from scratch, you'll have both the satisfaction of knowing it's carefully constructed and the opportunity to individualize your pickets.

MATERIALS

Masking tape or ribbon

Strips of cloth

¾-inch gravel

4 x 4 fence posts, 8-feet tall

2 x 4 rails, 6- or 8-feet long

No. 8 x 3-inch weatherized
deck screws

1 x 4 pickets, (cut from 10- or
12-foot lengths of pressure-
treated stock)

No 8 x 1¾-inch weatherized
deck screws

TOOLS AND SUPPLIES

Tape measure

1 x 2 stakes, 12-inches tall

Mason's line

Line level

Plumb bob

Posthole digger

Pencil

Combination square

Circular saw

Handsaw (optional, see step 4)

Jigsaw (optional, see steps 4 and 10)

Marking gauge

¾-inch mortise chisel

Wooden mallet

Carpenter's level

Cordless drill

Spring clamps

Table saw (optional, see step 11)

THE FOLLOWING MATERIALS ARE NECESSARY IF SETTING POSTS IN CONCRETE:

Concrete

Wheelbarrow

Shovel

Water

16d galvanized nails

Trowel

TIPS

■ Use only pressure-treated lumber or naturally decay-resistant wood (such as cedar, redwood, locust, osage orange, or cypress) for your fence. Because pressure-treated wood contains the preservative CCA (chromated copper arsenate), wear work gloves when handling it, and add a dust mask and protective eyewear when cutting it.

■ To determine the exact space between each picket, first decide approximately how much space you want between pickets, based on how dense you wish the fence to look. Add the picket and space width together, and divide the result into the total distance between the post centers. Round this to the nearest whole number. Multiply this number by the picket width to figure out the amount of space the pickets will occupy. Subtract that number from the distance between post centers. This tells you how much space is left for the spaces between the pickets. Divide this by the whole number determined above. (The completed fence will have one more picket than space.) This will give you the width of each space between pickets.

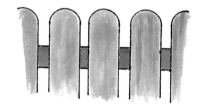
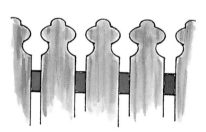

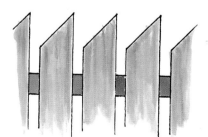

FIGURE 1. Picket fence styles

INSTRUCTIONS

1 Lay out your fence by measuring a distance along your intended line and driving 1 x 2 stakes into the ground to indicate the location of your two end posts. It will simplify matters later if you make the distance between the end posts a multiple of your rail length, typically 6 or 8 feet. Then drive two more stakes into the ground, each about 2 feet back from an end-post stake. Stretch mason's line between the two outermost stakes, with a line level attached at the midpoint. Make sure the line is taut and level.

2 Measure along the line between the end-post stakes and divide the total distance by the length of each fence section. For example, if your total run is 40 feet and you've planned 8-foot sections, you can fit five sections within the run, and you'll need six postholes. Use masking tape or ribbon to mark the locations along the mason's line where each post will fall. Then hang a plumb bob alongside each ribbon and mark that point on the ground with a nail and a strip of cloth. Use the posthole digger to excavate the individual postholes to a depth of 3 feet, centered at the marked points.

3 Now you can prepare the 4 x 4 fence posts, which can range in length from 72 to 96 inches, depending on your design. Given a level site, it's simpler and more accurate to mark and cut any post-top decorations or notched dadoes into the posts prior to setting them. Using the top of the post as a reference, measure down to the point where the upper edge of the top rail will go (between 4 and 13 inches), mark with the combination square, then measure to where the bottom of that rail will go, and mark. The distance between the marks should equal the width of the rail boards (3½ inches for 2 x 4s set on edge—typical rail boards). Then, measure down to the top of the planned lower rail (between 30 and 52 inches), and make similar marks for it. Repeat for all the posts.

NOTE: As an alternative, experienced woodworkers can set all the posts and then mark and cut them for horizontal rails after the posts are installed. Depending on the design, and how enduring you wish the fence to be, the rails don't necessarily have to be set in notches; they can be fastened to the surface of the posts with No. 8 x 3-inch weatherized deck screws for a quick and easy installation.

4 Mark and cut any post-top details you have planned. These could include a simple 45° bevel cut, a two- or four-sided 45° point, or an intricate jigsaw-cut finial pattern. A handsaw or circular saw will make a straight and easy cut.

5 Use a marking gauge to measure the depth of the notches—called dadoes—you intend to cut into the posts. These should equal the thickness of the rail boards, or 1½ inches. Once that's completed, set your circular saw to that depth and cut along the shoulder lines of each notch to define the opening. Then continue to make a series of parallel saw cuts through the wood between the shoulder cuts.

6 Using a ¾-inch mortise chisel and a wooden mallet, remove the waste material from the dadoes. Clean and smooth the bottom of each dado with the sharp edge of the chisel.

7 Set the end posts in place, following the procedure described in Setting Fence Posts, on page 62. Make sure, if you're bedding the rails in dadoes, that the slots all face the right direction.(Whether the dadoes and rails will be at the front or back of your fence depends on your design.) Set the mason's line to indicate the height of the bottom shoulder of the lower dadoes. Use a carpenter's level to plumb the posts; then backfill the holes.

8 Using the mason's line as a guide, set the line posts in place at the proper height, then plumb in both directions and backfill them.

9 Measure the center-to-center distance between each post as a double check prior to cutting the rails. Then trim the rails to the proper length. Each rail should butt the one next to it at the midpoint of the post. If that's not the case, minor adjustments can be made by trimming the rails slightly—but remember that they must abut at a post for support, and that changes in the length of the rails will affect the picket spacing. Use No. 8 x 3-inch weatherized deck screws to fasten both the upper and lower sets of rails to the posts.

10 Use a handsaw or circular saw to cut the 1 x 4 pickets from 10- or 12-foot straight lengths of pressure-treated stock. Once the overall lengths are cut, the picket style—ranging from straight-cut oblique or two-sided point to curved-cut round tops or spades (see figure 1, page 73)—can be added to the ends by cutting with a jigsaw. When cutting your own pickets, it's easier to clamp two or three together and cut as one than to go individually.

11 Positioning the pickets will be easier with a spacing gauge. To make one, first measure the distance between the top of the top rail and the bottom of the bottom rail. Add this number to the distance you'd like your pickets to extend below the

bottom rail. Then add ¾-inches to that number. Now cut a 1 x 4 to that length. Next, use the table saw to rip the board so that its width is equal to the desired space between pickets. Nail a piece of 1 x 4 level with the top of the board (as shown in figure 2).

12 Mark a line on the face of the first post to indicate the bottom of the pickets. Position the first picket on the line; then center and plumb it. Fasten it with No. 8 x 1¾-inch weatherized deck screws. Set the spacer gauge against the edge of the picket with its crosspiece facing outward. Position the second picket to match the height of the first, and fasten it to the upper and lower rails with two screws at each joint. Reverse the gauge, as shown in figure 2, to continue mounting the remaining pickets.

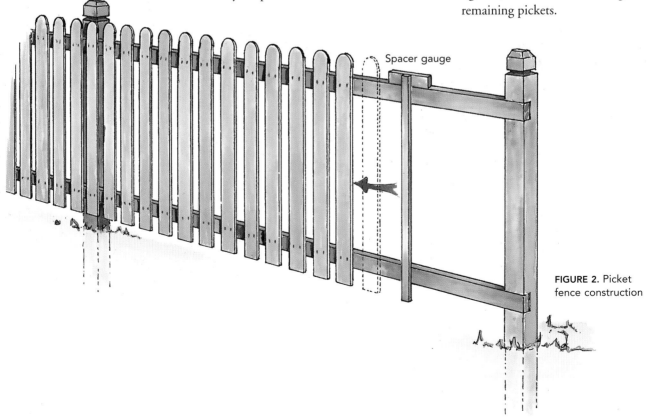

Spacer gauge

FIGURE 2. Picket fence construction

project

Living Willow Fence

ere's a fence you can build without a hammer or nails. Woven from willow, this border may actually take root, sprout leaves (and pussywillows!), and become a living lattice fence. The best time of year to make this fence is early spring, right before the willow breaks its dormancy.

MATERIALS

Willow (see Tip)

Twine

TOOLS AND SUPPLIES

Two stakes

String or mason's line

Spading fork

Loppers

TIP

■ Willow whips (young willow shoots without any branches) can be purchased from suppliers, but in many places it's possible to gather your own willow (you may need to trim branches) from riverbanks and roadsides. Always ask permission before gathering from private property.

INSTRUCTIONS

1 Lay out the fence line with two stakes and string or mason's line.

2 Use the spading fork to cultivate a 30-inch-wide trench along the fence line to a depth of about 6 inches. Add compost or composted manure to the trench.

3 Starting on the right end of your fence line, insert the willows whips into the trench so each one is leaning to the left at a 45° angle. The whips should be inserted to a depth of 4 to 6 inches, and spaced about 8 inches apart.

4 Repeat step 3 at the left end of your fence line, only this time each willow whip should angle to the right and be inserted at a midpoint between two of the left-leaning whips planted in step 3. Plant these whips so that they cross just slightly in front of the whips going in the opposite direction.

5 Insert one vertical whip at each end of your fence line.

6 Standing to one side of the fence, begin gently weaving in the simple over and under, diamond pattern shown in figure 1. This will be easiest if you work your way up the fence, weaving one section, rather than one willow whip, at a time. It's important to replace any whips that break or crack, or that section of fence may die or become diseased. When you get to the end of the fence line, you can trim the ends that extend out past the vertical whips, or you can gently wrap them around the vertical whip and weave them back into the fence's pattern, as shown in figure 1.

7 Tie each intersection loosely with twine.

8 Water your fence daily for the first growing season. Once the fence is established and growing well (toward the end of the first growing season), use loppers to trim the top and shape the fence.

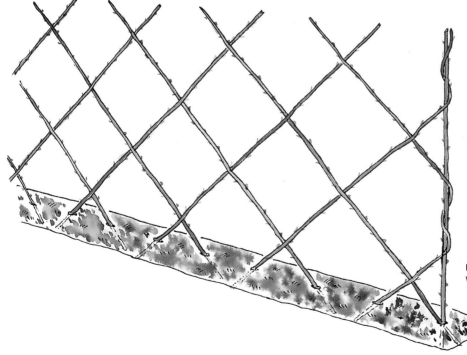

FIGURE 1.
Woven willow fence

Hedges and Tall Plantings

chapter

4

HEDGES ARE LIVING BORDERS. AND LIKE MOST LIVING THINGS, they can try your patience. You must wait patiently for a hedge to reach the desired height. You'll need to patiently prune a hedge if it's to resemble a wall instead of a forest. But how that patience will be rewarded! Hedges grown tall and dense enough will provide privacy, security, and shade to your property. They'll define and shape a garden, while buffering wind, absorbing noise, and filtering dust and pollutants. Hedges can even provide a habitat for birds and other wildlife. If you start with young plants (which generally transplant best), a hedge should be less expensive than a wall or fence of the same length. And planting a hedge is almost always easier and faster than building a wall or fence.

A hedge is not, however, something to plant on impulse. Make sure first that the hedge you have in mind will suit your needs. Could your pet work its way beneath the greenery each time it tries to make a break for freedom? (Thorny plants might help here.) Are you going to be happy with the skeletal appearance of a deciduous hedge when those blossoms (and all the foliage) have made their annual departure? And do you really have the time and patience (and water!) to nurture those individual plants toward hedgedom?

If you do decide that a hedge is the right border for you, you still need to stop and consider carefully exactly which kind of hedge is best for your situation. Practically every neighborhood has a straggly, overgrown hedge or two that have gotten away from their owners. Research carefully the mature height and width of any shrub before you plant, and be sure to site the hedge a safe distance from any property lines to accommodate unexpected growth. Be realistic about the amount of time you have to maintain your hedge. You may find that an alternative to traditional hedges works better for you. Information is included here about tall ornamental grasses that can be used as a low-maintenance screen in your yard and tall annuals that can provide summertime shade and privacy while a hedge is becoming established.

Formal Hedges

Formal hedges are civilized. Instead of shouting, "Keep Out!", they seem to command, in a headmasterly tone, that one should stay within the pre-scribed limits of their crisp, green lines. The living architecture of a formal hedge reminds us that a human has had a hand in this garden, a very patient human who has planted with an eye to the future.

Made up of shrubs (usually ever-green), spaced and shaped so that individual plants become lost in the overall design, formal hedges require a

PLANTS FOR FORMAL HEDGES

Arborvitae
Thuja

Barberry
Berberis

Boxwood
Buxus

Inkberry
Ilex glabra

Japanese holly
Ilex crenata

Juniper
Juniperus

Privet
Ligustrum

Red-tip photinia
Photinia x fraseri

Sweet bay
Laurus nobilis

Yew
Taxus

planting site that offers consistent growing conditions. If one end of your yard is sunny and dry and the other end stays moist and shady, you're going to have difficulty growing a formal hedge across its expanse. Formal hedges also require a fairly wide site, since they fill more space than walls or fences. Add to that their need for conscientious and continual pruning, and vigilance against pests and diseases, and you can see this is a high-maintenance border.

But in return, a formal hedge can bring much more than its stately beauty to your yard. Low formal hedges both decorate and divide yards and gardens, sometimes in straightforward lines, sometime in intricate patterns. They're excellent for directing traffic, enclosing a patio, or establishing a low border between the front yard and the street. Tall formal hedges provide privacy. A gated formal hedge can make your yard secure if its branches grow low enough to the ground and the hedge is both tall and dense enough. (Dense hedges grown from thorny shrubs offer the best security.) Formal hedges can also temper strong winds, reduce noise, and filter dust and pollutants. The solid green of a formal hedge creates the perfect backdrop for flower beds and gives structure to your landscape, even in winter. The cost of a formal hedge will depend on the age and species of plants used. If started with young plants, the cost—compared to a wall or fence of the same size—should be modest. Fast-growing species will reach their full height quicker, but they'll also require more frequent pruning.

Informal Hedges

If you're sold on the benefits of a hedge, but you think a formal one might be a bit pretentious for your setting (or a bit demanding for your schedule), consider an informal hedge. These hedges fit in with a variety of architectural and gardening styles, and they require far less pruning than formally shaped hedges. They do tend to spread wider than their carefully pruned formal cousins though, so make sure you have room on your property for a mature hedge of this type. (Because they're not closely clipped like formal hedges, informal hedges should not be planted close to paths and walkways, especially if they contain thorny plants, such as roses.)

Informal hedges can consist of a single species or a carefully combined tapestry of mixed shrubs. They can offer the beauty and fragrance of blossoms or an ever-changing wall of color and texture. Informal hedges made up of a single species will, like formal hedges, look best if grown where site conditions remain consistent. Like formal hedges, they also carry the danger of the entire planting succumbing to attack from pests or disease. Mixed hedges, on the other hand, work well in sites where sunlight or soil conditions vary. Their diversity helps them fight off insect attacks and disease and makes the replacement of a dead plant less noticeable.

The functions an informal hedge can serve in your yard or garden will depend, in large measure, on the species planted. Before choosing plants for an informal hedge, review the information in the first chapter and remind yourself of the main reasons you need a border. Remember that deciduous shrubs, while often pro-

viding welcome blooms in spring and summer, will offer little privacy in winter. And, while many deciduous shrubs have handsome bark or interesting structures, some look downright depressing when striped of foliage. This may not be a problem in the backyard or if your hedge will be covered with snow all winter. But naked, forlorn branches lining your front yard will only add to the gloom of winter.

As with a formal hedge, the cost of an informal hedge will depend primarily on the type and size of the plants used. Informal hedges don't need to be sheared, but they do require pruning at least once a year to remove dead or weak shoots and to maintain the shrubs' basic shapes.

PLANTS FOR INFORMAL HEDGES

Bigleaf hydrangea
Hydrangea macrophylla

Border forsythia
Forsythia x intermedia

Carolina allspice
Calycanthus floridus

Glossy abelia
Abelia x grandiflora

Japanese maple
Acer plamatum

Lilac
Syringa vulgaris

Mountain laurel
Kalmia latifolia

Rhododendron
Rhododendron

Rose
Rosa

Witch hazel
Hamamelis

Ornamental grasses can serve as a seasonal border.

Ornamental Grasses

Ornamental grasses offer a fast-growing alternative to shrubs. Inexpensive to plant and practically maintenance-free, ornamental grasses can create a living border that dances in the breeze, changes color with the seasons, and looks attractive year round. Erect grasses that aren't prone to flopping and will grow at least 5 feet tall are the best choice for borders. Your local nursery should be able to tell you the types that are best suited to your area and to your yard's growing conditions. Most grasses will take only two to three years to reach their full size.

Use a screen of ornamental grasses to form an internal boundary in your yard and to provide privacy and dappled shade. The cost of a grass border should be moderate to inexpensive. Best of all, borders made up of tall ornamental grasses are practically maintenance-free. Other than regular watering until they become established and one crewcut sometime between late fall and early spring, grasses require almost no care. Some ornamental grasses are invasive, so check that this is not the case with any species you're thinking of planting. Keep in mind that these self-reliant plants are stubborn; digging up an established bed of tall grasses is a daunting task, so think carefully before deciding where to locate such a border.

Tall Annuals

A dense row of tall flowering annuals can serve as a stunning substitute for a conventional hedge. This cheerful blooming border can provide you with cut flowers for indoors and help attract birds and butterflies, while bringing summertime privacy and shade to your yard. Plant one in front of a slow-growing hedge or to help you visualize what a more permanent border could do for your property.

A closely planted row or two of tall bushy annuals works best—choose plants that stay erect without staking. Dramatic effects can be achieved by planting a single species or you can mix different flowers for a colorful composition. Growing a tall screen of flowering annuals is a great way to enclose a patio or separate a children's play area from the vegetable garden.

Tall spider flowers provide a screen of summer color in this handsome garden.

Pruning Hedges

HOW YOU PRUNE A HEDGE DEPENDS ON WHETHER the hedge is formal or informal and the type of plant (or plants) used in the hedge. While proper pruning can improve both the appearance and the health of your hedge, improper pruning can weaken or even kill it. Therefore, you should research the pruning requirements of the specific shrub variety (or varieties) that makes up your hedge. The following should serve as general guidelines to hedge pruning.

Initial Pruning

Because you want your hedge to grow bigger and pruning seems to (at least initially) make it smaller, you may be tempted to hold off until the shrubs have reached the desired height for a hedge. But this is a mistake. Shrubs left to grow up without pruning will have long, weak stems that branch out only at their tips. These stems may snap in a heavy wind, rain, or snow. Bare-root shrubs should be pruned back hard (cut to one-third to one-half their height) when planted so they will begin to bush out. Container-grown or balled-and-burlapped shrubs can be pruned only to remove dead wood at the initial planting.

Regular Pruning

After the initial pruning, the pruning methods for hedges differ completely for formal and informal hedges. That is because you're trying to accomplish two very different things. With formal hedges, you're pruning in order to force your shrubs to maintain an unnatural shape. With informal hedges, you prune to enhance both the shrubs' health and their natural shapes.

FORMAL HEDGES

Formal Hedges are sheared, which means removing just a few inches of growth off the top and sides of the hedge's surface without ever cutting into hardened-off wood (see figure 1). It's a little like mowing your lawn, and just as grass does not naturally grow short and tidy, shrubs don't naturally grow into perfectly shaped rectangles or orbs. The inside of a formally sheared hedge usually contains a good deal of dead wood, which means this kind of hedge is vulnerable to damage from insects, disease, and heavy wind, rain, and snow.

The shrubs for formal hedges need to be shaped by shearing as soon as they begin to grow. Hedge shears with sharp blades will work well when the shrubs are young and have not yet started mingling into a hedge. Once they have become an established hedge, you may find an electric hedge trimmer to be more efficient. (Whichever tool you use, make sure the blades are sharp so they cut the branches instead of tearing them.) Continuous pruning will increase the amount of time it takes for your hedge to reach its full

FIGURE 1. Sheared hedge

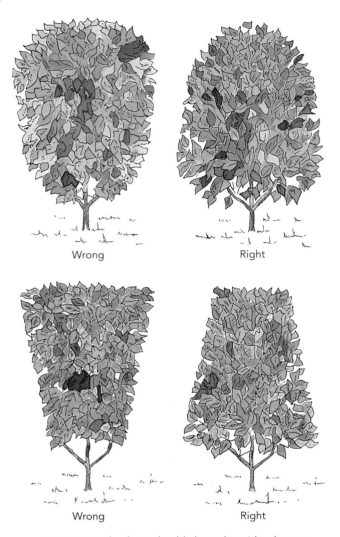

Wrong   Right

Wrong   Right

FIGURE 2. Hedge base should always be wider than top.

height, but it will also result in a healthier, longer-lived hedge. It's important, even from the beginning, to cut your hedge at a slight angle so its base is a bit wider than the rest of it (see figure 2). Otherwise, sunlight won't be able to reach all the branches and the lowest ones will die.

How often you need to shear your formal hedge will depend on the species grown and the shape you're trying to maintain. Shearing can usually take place anytime between late fall to midsummer. If you live in an area where frost might damage new growth, don't shear in late summer or early fall. You can use a template cut from plywood as a guide, or string stretched taut between two posts.

INFORMAL HEDGES

Informal hedges are thinned rather than sheared. While shearing takes place on the surface of the shrub, thinning involves reaching down inside the plant to thin out weak or dead branches and to improve light and air penetration (see figure 3). With thinning, you try to maintain the natural shape of each shrub as you prune.

Sharp bypass pruners should be used for growth ¾-inch in diameter or smaller. Loppers work best on branches up to 2-inches in diameter. Branches bigger than that will probably require a pruning saw. Begin thinning by cutting all dead and weak shoots or limbs to their points of origins or to ground level. Branches that are damaged, are growing in toward the center of the shrub, or are crossing and rubbing against another branch should be cut in the same manner. (When branches are rubbing, cut the smaller of the two.) You can also cut to help shape the shrub, but remember, your goal here is to have a healthy plant with a shape that's both pleasing and natural.

The best time for thinning a hedge is when the plants are dormant (the time between when the leaves fall in autumn and when new growth appears in spring). Don't thin in late summer to early fall or you'll encourage new growth that will be susceptible to frost damage.

FIGURE 3. Thinned hedge

project

Formal Hedge

Want to add order and elegance to your yard? Do you like taking control of your surroundings? A formal hedge may be just the border for you. The crisp, green architecture of a formal hedge will provide a living border that can set boundaries and provide privacy and security, while buffering winds, absorbing noise, and screening out dust and pollution.

MATERIALS

Compost or soil amendments
Shrubs (see Tips)
Mulch

TOOLS AND SUPPLIES

String
2 stakes
Hose
Gardening spade
Gardening fork

TIPS

■ Plant bare-root shrubs in late fall to early spring, while the plants are still dormant. Container-grown or balled-and-burlapped hedge plants can be set out anytime during the growing season but will require abundant watering in summer.

■ For a formal hedge, it's important to start with young plants that are all from the same supplier and have been propagated from a single stock.

■ If you have room on your property, consider growing a few extra plants from the same stock to have on hand in case a plant in your hedge is damaged or doesn't grow properly.

INSTRUCTIONS

1 Tie the string to the two stakes and use it to mark out a straight line for your hedge. If planting a curved hedge, use a garden hose to outline the desired shape.

2 Dig a trench along this line that's as deep as the plants' roots and approximately twice as wide as the plants' root balls or containers. (Be sure to reserve the excavated soil for later use.)

3 Carefully unwind the roots of pot-bound plants, and prune any roots that are damaged. Remove twine or wire from balled-and-burlapped plants, and pull the burlap away from the trunk. Genuine burlap in a single layer can be left to decompose; anything else should be removed. Set your plants into the trench at the recommended planting distance. (Remember, this is the planting distance to create a dense hedge—it will be much closer than the typical planting distance for shrubs.) If the quality of your plants varies, alternate stronger and weaker plants in the row, as shown in figure 1.

4 Use the excavated soil (mixed with compost or soil amendments, if needed) to refill the trench halfway. Check the spacing and the alignment of the plants, and make any necessary adjustments. Then water thoroughly. When the water has drained, fill the trench to the top with the remaining soil and tamp down. Then water thoroughly once again.

5 To preserve moisture and prevent weed growth, spread a 3-inch layer of mulch around each shrub, taking care to keep the mulch several inches away from the plants' trunks. Water well (every three to five days) for the first month, and then water weekly for the first one or two growing seasons.

6 Don't wait until the hedge has grown to the size desired before beginning to prune and shape. (see page 86 for general information on pruning.) The nursery where you purchased your plants should also be able to provide guidance for your particular plants and style of hedge.

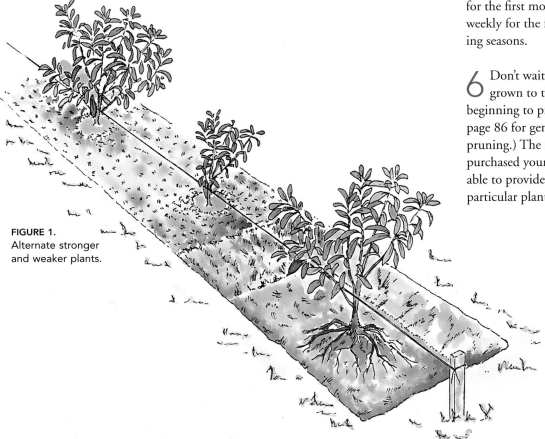

FIGURE 1.
Alternate stronger and weaker plants.

Informal Hedge

f the style of your yard (or your pruning schedule) is on the relaxed side, consider an informal hedge. Informal hedges usually fill out faster than formal hedges, and they often carry the bonus of flowers and fragrance. Although an informal hedge of just one species can be stunning, a mixed hedge that combines different species can offer a rich display of color and texture that will vary throughout the year.

MATERIALS

Compost or soil amendments

Shrubs (see Tips)

Mulch

TOOLS AND SUPPLIES

String

2 stakes

Hose

Gardening spade

Gardening fork

TIPS

■ If you're planting a mixed hedge, be sure to consider the required growing conditions, rate of growth, and mature height and width of each plant. In a hedge with both evergreen and deciduous shrubs, consider placement carefully, so the effect will still be pleasing in winter.

■ If you're starting your hedge with bare-root plants, plant them in late fall to early spring, while they're still dormant. Container-grown or balled-and-burlapped plants can be set out anytime during the growing season but will require abundant watering in summer.

■ The nursery where you buy your shrubs should be able to tell you the plants' mature spread. The planting distance for most shrubs will be about two-thirds the distance of their mature spread (slow growers can be planted closer—about one-half the distance of their mature spread).

The lilacs lining this yard provide a fragrant informal hedge.

INSTRUCTIONS

1 Use the string and stakes or a garden hose to lay out the line of your hedge. Informal hedges are typically planted in looser formations than formal hedges, especially if made up of different species.

2 Shrubs for informal hedges can be planted in a trench (follow the directions for planting a formal hedge, page 88) or in individual holes. Holes should be as deep as the plant's roots and approximately twice as wide as the plant's root ball or container. Your gardening spade can serve as a depth gauge if you mark the handle to show the height of the root ball and then use the mark to determine the proper depth for your hole (see figures 1 and 2).

3 Carefully unwind the roots of pot-bound plants, and prune any roots that are damaged. Remove twine or wire from balled-and-burlapped plants, and pull the burlap away from the trunk. Genuine burlap in a single layer can be left to decompose; anything else should be removed. Set your plants into the trench or holes at the recommend planting distance.

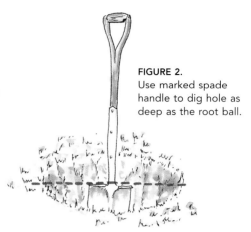

FIGURE 2.
Use marked spade handle to dig hole as deep as the root ball.

4 Use the excavated soil (mixed with compost or soil amendments, if needed) to refill the trench or hole halfway, and then water thoroughly. Allow the water to drain; then fill the trench or hole to the top with the remaining soil. Adjust plants if necessary, and tamp down the soil. Then water thoroughly once again.

5 To conserve moisture and prevent weed growth, spread a 3-inch layer of mulch around each shrub, taking care to keep mulch several inches away from the shrubs' trunks. Water well (every three to five days) for the first month, and then water weekly for the first one or two growing seasons.

6 Even shrubs for informal hedges usually need pruning to encourage them to fill out nicely (see page 86 for general information on pruning.) The nursery where you purchased your plants should be able to provide guidance for your particular plants.

FIGURE 1.
Mark your spade handle at the root ball height.

project

Simple Sunflower Border

A row of bright, cheerful sunflowers is certain to bring smiles to the faces of everyone passing by. Planting such a screen is one of the simplest ways to add a tall (if temporary) border to your yard. An amazing variety of sunflowers is available these days, so finding the look and height that's right for your setting will be easy. Take advantage of the low cost of this unconventional hedge and plant generously—you'll want cut flowers to bring inside and plenty of seed to share with the birds.

MATERIALS

Sunflower seeds
Seed pots (optional, see Tips)
Seed-starting mix (optional, see Tips)
Compost
Mulch

TOOLS AND SUPPLIES

Gardening spade

TIPS

■ You can give your sunflower border a head start by starting seeds indoors in seed pots and seed-starting mix, six to eight weeks before the last frost date for your area.

■ In general, sunflowers require full sun and well-drained soil. Their flowers will usually face east to southeast. Some varieties can reach up to 15 feet in height, so be sure to grow them where they won't cast shade onto other sun-loving plants. Also, if your border will have more than one variety, make sure the tallest types get planted at the back of the border.

INSTRUCTIONS

1 After the last spring frost, use the gardening spade to cultivate a 1- to 2-foot wide planting strip about 6 inches deep. If you're planning to grow a double row of sunflowers, you will, of course, need a wider planting strip. Add in compost to aid soil drainage.

2 Plant seeds 1 to 1½ inches below the soil, 6 inches apart. Make sure the seeds are covered with soil, or birds will snack on them. Water well, and then keep soil slightly moist until the seeds germinate, usually in 10 to 14 days.

3 When the seedlings have four leaves, thin them to the planting distance recommended on the seed packet (this will depend on the variety).

4 Once the plants are growing well, add a layer of mulch to help the soil retain moisture and to discourage weeds. Now you can begin to water less frequently, but always water deeply. Doing so will encourage the roots to explore deep down into the soil, which will make the plants less likely to need staking.

5 Plants and Borders

ADD A WALL, FENCE, OR HEDGE TO YOUR YARD, and you've suddenly got more planting sites. Truth be told, that was my sole reason for building a picket fence in my front yard. I'd already planted every part of the front that made sense and every part of the backyard that hadn't been claimed by husband, child, or dog. But I still wanted to grow climbing roses, foxgloves, lady's-mantle, and a combination of purple coneflowers and gayfeather I'd once seen in a magazine. Forgo new clothes, jewelry, and a fancy car, and you can justify the expense of a gardening obsession, but what do you do when your square feet of ground can no longer support your habit? Grow up! A mere 30 feet of picket fence gave me a structure for roses to climb up and over and justification to start two new flower beds: full-sun plants on one side and partial-shade plants on the other.

Of course, most people build or plant a border for all the practical reasons explored in the first chapter (if you're a gardening addict, feel free to choose any of those reasons so you, too, can appear practical). But then they realize that their newly erected fence looks stark. Something's missing. It's crying out for blossoms at its base or a blanket of vines growing up and over it, plants that will soften the hard architecture of a border so it blends in and becomes a part of the landscape.

Borders not only need plants—plants, too, often need borders. The diaphanous *Daucus carota* (Queen Anne's lace to most of us) that might get lost in the middle of an island bed will pop into focus when you provide the backdrop of a wall, fence, or hedge. Similarly, a flower bed that looks forlorn and bare in winter can be anchored by a wall, fence, or hedge. As long as you carefully match your plants to your site, borders can also enable you to grow plants that don't typically grow in your climate.

Growing Conditions

When I built that picket fence, I created partial shade in my front yard where before there was full sun all day. The first thing you must remember is that adding a wall, fence, or hedge will alter the growing conditions of your site. How happy the marriage between your border and your new plants will turn out to be will depend in large measure on how carefully you consider site conditions before choosing your plants.

SOIL

Stroll outside after a rain storm and look at the ground below your wall, fence, or hedge—you'll see a dry area extending out along the base, a *rain shadow*. This sheltered section of soil won't receive the same amount of rain as the open areas of your garden. If the border that casts the rain shadow is a brick wall or a hedge, even more moisture will be sucked up out of the ground. Because of this, you should always plant 12 to 18 inches out from your border. Cultivating the soil deeply, adding in plenty of organic material, and keeping plants well-mulched should also help combat the dryness of a rain shadow.

Along with stealing moisture, hedges will also rob the soil of nutrients, so anything growing beside a hedge will need extra fertilizer unless it's a plant (such as nasturtium) that flowers better in poor soil. Walls built from limestone or with lime in their mortar or stucco may leach lime into the soil, making it alkaline and therefore unfit for plants such as rhododendrons and camellias. Rosemary, on the other hand, would be quite content in a dry, unfertile soil with some lime in it.

The soil at the top of a wall tends to dry out quickly.

Success depends on matching plants to site conditions.

PLANTING POINTERS

Along with the growing conditions of your site, keep the following points in mind when cultivating the area around your border.

■ Obvious as it seems, it can be hard to remember to position plants so that the tallest ones are closest to the border and the shortest ones are at the front of the bed.

■ Tall plants situated close to a wall, fence, or hedge will lean forward to get more sunlight, so they may need to be staked.

■ Keep in mind the mature size of trees and shrubs when planting them near borders.

■ Don't grow plants prone to mildew or fungal diseases too close to a solid wall or fence, especially in humid climates.

■ Consider the color and texture of your wall, fence, or hedge when choosing your plants. With a hedge, you also need to consider its foliage color throughout the year and whether it's deciduous or evergreen. (See page 116 for more on borders and color.)

SUN

Every vertical element in your garden will have a sunny side and a shady side. The plants on the sunny side of a wall or fence will receive not only sun but also plenty of heat in summer. They'll get both the heat from the sun and that reflected back from the structure. (The amount of heat will depend on the wall or fence's orientation, the construction and finish materials used, and your local cli-

mate.) Heat-loving, drought-tolerant plants, such as lavender or sunflower, would do well on the south side of a fence or wall with an east-west orientation. This is also the place to try sun-loving tender perennials that normally aren't hardy in your area.

This is *not* the case, however, if your fence or wall is located at the bottom of a slope. Cold air—like water—flows downhill, and if it's

trapped by a solid structure, a frost pocket can occur. A wall or fence with an open design or a hedge would work better in this situation. If you can't avoid having a solid fence or wall at the bottom of a slope, then you'll have to choose plants that can tolerate the cold (this depends, in part, on your climate) or plants that don't poke their heads out of the ground until late spring when all danger of frost is past.

A border that receives full sun is an opportunity to plant colorful combinations.

PLANTS FOR DRY, SUNNY SITES

Blanket flower
Gaillardia

Daylily
Hemerocallis

Gayfeather
Liatris

Lantana
Lantana camara

Lavender
Lavandula

Sage
Salvia

Sunflower
Helianthus

Mexican sunflower
Tithonia rotundifolia

Yarrow
Achillea

Zinnia
Zinnia

PLANTS FOR DRY, SHADY SITES

Boxwood
Buxus

Bugleweed
Ajuga reptans

Cotoneaster
Cotoneaster

Creeping juniper
Juniperus horizontalis

Lamb's-ears
Stachys byzantina

Liriope
Liriope muscari

Pearly everlasting
Anaphalis margaritacea

Periwinkle
Vinca

Plumbago
Ceratostigma plumbaginoides

Stinking iris
Iris foetidissima

SHADE

When I first started gardening, my feelings toward shade plants were like those of most kids toward vegetables—a necessary evil on the path to dessert (or, in my case, bright, sun-loving flowers). As my tastes have matured and I've come to appreciate the subtler beauty in the texture of a large-leafed blue hosta or the intricate fronds of a fern, all the formerly neglected parts of my yard have come to life. And on a hot summer afternoon I'm only too happy to be puttering on the shady side of the fence. It's not only cooler there, but it also needs less water (except for the rain shadow), less mulch, weeding, pruning, and (with the exception of slugs) less pest patrol.

Dry shade *can* be difficult to grow plants in. It took three years for me to admit that, all good intentions aside, I was not going to manage to constantly water the moisture-loving primroses I was determined to grow in the dry shade beside a wall in my backyard. The cheerful periwinkle that grows there now looks so much better than the bed of dried, dead stems I inevitably wound up with each summer.

If your wall, fence, or hedge doesn't receive full sun, explore the many beautiful shade plants available.

Growing Plants up and over a Border

The sight of a new, bare wall or fence can be as tempting to a gardener as a freshly plowed acre. But before you rush to the nursery with visions of climbing roses, clematis, and sweet peas in your head, research the plants you're considering. Along with their preferred growing conditions, you also need to know how they attach (or don't attach) to vertical surfaces. Do they cling, scramble, twine, or use tendrils?

TOP, RIGHT: Self-clinging ivy needs no support to work its way up this stone wall.

ABOVE: The rose, clematis, and honeysuckle have each used a different method to climb this picket fence.

TYPES OF CLIMBERS

Self-clinging plants are the mountaineers of vines. They are divided into two types. Self-clingers such as ivy and climbing hydrangea employ aerial roots that exude a sort of glue to stick to walls and fences. The other type of self-clinger has tendrils with little discs on the ends that stick to wood, stone, or cement (Virginia creeper is an example of this type). *Twining* plants, such as morning glories, grow by wrapping their leading shoots up and around a vertical support, always twining clockwise or counterclockwise, depending on the species. Vines that climb with *tendrils* (or in some cases, modified leaf stalks) reach out and grab ahold of any available support to hoist themselves up. Sweet peas and passion-flowers are examples of this kind of vine. The plants that need the most help to grow vertically are *climbers*. Climbers (climbing roses are an example) are not true vines but are either plants with long stems that lean over and sometimes use thorns to catch on surfaces, or they are *scandent* plants (those with flexible stems that will grow over or through supports but have no real means of self-attachment).

SUPPORT FOR CLIMBERS

It's important to have your support system in place when you plant your climber; otherwise, you'll inevitably damage the plant. Before you erect the support system, make certain your wall or fence is sturdy enough for your vine and is in good repair—maintenance will be difficult once the climber is established. A formal hedge generally does not work well as a support for a climber because it has to be pruned constantly.

The type of support your vine will need depends on its climbing method and its size when mature. No support

TOP, RIGHT: Tendril climbers, such as these sweet peas, need slender supports to grab.

ABOVE: Morning glories climb by twining.

is necessary for self-clingers; they'll attach themselves right to most surfaces. This, of course, is great when it's the same surface you had in mind. It's less wonderful when they decide to go exploring on their own. The rootlets and discs can be difficult to remove, so grow self-clingers only where you're sure you want them, and plan on pruning them regularly to keep them contained. Avoid these vines on walls with cracks or crumbling mortar where they may cause damage. Also, because clinging evergreens tend to collect moisture, they can cause problems on wooden fences.

Twining and tendril-type vines can work their way up most ornamental metal and chain-link fences without any additional support. They may also be able to climb up lattice (or other open style) fences if parts of the framework are slender enough for the vines or tendrils to coil around. On fences where this is not the case and on most walls, you'll need to attach plastic or wire mesh (dark colors look

CLIMBERS AND VINES FOR SUN

Black-eyed Susan vine
Thunbergia alata

Cup-and-saucer vine
Cobaea scandens

Grapevine
Vitis

Moonflower
Ipomoea alba

Morning glory
Ipomoea

Rose
Rosa

Scarlet runner bean
Phaseolus coccineus

Sweet pea
Lathyrus odoratus

Trumpet vine
Campsis radicans

Japanese wisteria
Wisteria floribunda

The bourbon climbing rose 'Reine Victoria' doesn't actually climb, but it will grow up (and sprawl over) borders.

CLIMBERS AND VINES FOR SHADE

Boston ivy
Parthenocissus tricuspidata

Carolina jasmine
Gelsemium sempervirens

Climbing hydrangea
Hydrangea anomala

Creeping fig
Ficus pumila

Dutchman's-pipe
Aristolochia durior

Five-leaf akebia
Akebia quinata

Hardy kiwi
Actinidia kolomikta

Ivy
Hedera helix

Sweet autumn clematis
Clematis maximowicziana

Winter-flowering jasmine
Jasminum nudiflorum

best), galvanized wires, or a trellis. The size of the support should be suitable for the plant when young *and* when it reaches maturity. A morning glory can wrap itself around a length of twine or a thin bamboo pole just fine, but honeysuckle would quickly outgrow such supports. A truly vigorous twiner, such as wisteria, could crush some fences eventually. A vine with tendrils can usually work its way up a hedge on its own, but it needs appropriately sized wires or a trellis to get a leg up on a wall or fence. (The exception would be a chain-link or other fence with slender supports the tendrils could wrap themselves around.)

Climbers that aren't true vines, such as roses or cotoneaster, must be trained and attached to their supports as they grow. A low-tech method for this is to simply hammer rustproof nails into your wall or fence as needed and then tie the climber to the nails with flexible plant ties. Lead-headed nails have a stem attached to the head

that you can bend to hold a plant in place. Of course, the problem with using either type of nail is that you have to continually add new nails as the climber grows. It's easier to attach a permanent system such as wires or trellis and tie the stems onto that as they grow.

One of the best support systems for vines consists of galvanized wires attached to a wall or fence with vine eyes (or screw eyes) and anchors and then pulled taut. The wire can run vertically, horizontally, or diagonally. Many plants bloom best when they are trained horizontally on a fence or wall. Check to see whether this is true of the climber you have in mind. Vigorous climbers, such as silver lace vine and wisteria, require heavy-gauge wire. Whatever your vine, make certain the vine eyes hold the wire far enough out from the wall or fence to allow for ample air circulation.

Secure trellises, too, in a manner that provides adequate airflow between the plant-covered trellis and your border. This can be done by attaching treated 1 x 2s to the wall or fence first and then mounting the trellis onto the 1 x 2s. Use rustproof hinges to attach the trellis, and it will be easy to move it from the wall or fence when the border needs maintenance.

WARNING

The vine that looks so pretty as it meanders up your fence can all too quickly become the monster that devours your fence, trees, and house. That seemingly demure morning glory at the back of a flower bed might bring you to your knees (literally) next year when you have to weed the countless seedlings it has scattered everywhere. Vigorous vines planted too close to your house can cause damage to your eaves, gutters, and roof shingles. Because vines can vary widely in their habits, even within the same species, it's important to research the exact cultivar you're considering planting.

A number of non-native vines are causing damage to the environment in much of the United States. (Kudzu, perhaps the most famous rampant vine, has invaded Southeastern forests in square footage about equal in size to the state of Maryland.) Japanese honeysuckle (*Lonicera japonica*), porcelain berry vine (*Ampelopsis brevipedunculata*), Chinese wisteria (*Wisteria sinensis*), and climbing euonymus (*Euonymus fortunei*) are just a few of the vines that are out of control in parts of the United States. Contact your local Cooperative Extension Service to find out which vines are safe and unsafe to grow in your area.

Some vines (such as this trumpet vine) can take over a border.

Plants grow both on top of and out of this stone wall.

Growing Plants in Walls

Along with planting in front of and up walls, you can also plant right *in* retaining walls. Nature does this all the time; you may have noticed plants growing out of the tiniest cracks in stone walls. You can imitate this by planting in the cracks and crevices of your own wall. If your wall is built from local stone and you plant native plants in it, it will look right at home in its surroundings.

Be forewarned: getting plants to take root and grow in the tiny cracks and crevices of a wall is so rewarding, it can become addictive. Use restraint so the natural beauty of the stone still shows through. (Of course, if you've inherited an eyesore and your goal is to disguise the structure, then you can let loose and cover the wall with cascading plants.) Also, don't allow your enthusiasm for these gymnastic growers to entice you to remove a wall's rocks or large chunks of mortar—the wall could become unstable.

SUITABLE PLANTS

Before you decide what to grow in your retaining wall, ask yourself all the usual questions about growing conditions. Will the plants get full sun, partial shade, or full shade? How much moisture will the plants receive? (With dry stone retaining walls, which angle back to a bank, the soil tends to be dry at the top and stay moister at the bottom.) How windy is the site?

Fleabane (*Erigeron karvin-skianus*) thrives in the dry conditions of a rock wall, and it often reseeds in the tiniest of cracks.

Often the gaps between rocks in a wall create microclimates that will be more moderate (warmer in winter and cooler in summer) than what's typical for your area. So this may be a place to experiment with a plant that's not reliably hardy in your zone—prostrate rosemary, for instance. Drought-tolerant plants with small root systems, such as hens-and-chicks and other succulents; small creeping plants, such as woolly thyme; and tough reseeding annuals, such as lobelia and sweet alyssum, are all good candidates for these horticultural acrobatics.

PLANTS TO GROW IN A WALL

Candytuft
Iberis sempervirens

Ice plant
Delosperma aberdeenense

Hens-and-chicks
Sempervivum

Lavender cotton
Santolina chamaecyparissus

Pinks
Dianthus

Rock cress
Arabis caucasica

Snow-in-summer
Cerastium tomentosum

Thrift
Armeria

Wooly thyme
Thymus pseudolanuginosus

Yellow corydalis
Corydalis lutea

Thyme and sedum are growing on top of this wall; the sedum has managed to gain a foothold in the wall's small cracks.

PLANTING THE WALL

If you can, it's best to plant dry-stack stone retaining walls as you build them. That way you can make sure the plants have a trail of soil that extends all the way from the front of the wall back to the bank being retained. This will help the plants get adequate moisture. Planting as you build will also allow you to use larger plants with more developed root systems and to spread those root systems out to help the plant become established.

When you're building your wall and you get to a point where you'd like to have a plant, leave a space between two stones that's large enough to hold the plant's crown (the spot where the stem and root merge) plus soil. Set down a trail of loamy soil from the front of the wall all the way back to the bank. (You may want to put landscape fabric over the rubble and gravel backfill first to keep the soil there from washing away.) Lay the plant in the gap between the two stones so that its crown is 2 inches in from the front of the wall and its roots are spread out over the top of the soil. Add more soil on top of the roots, and water well. Then you can continue building the wall, eventually adding gravel backfill over the soil

that's covering the plant's roots. Water the plant regularly until it's established (generally one full growing season) and as needed after that.

If you already have a stone wall that you'd like to add plants to, your job will be a bit trickier. Try to find a crevice that extends far back into the wall, and press good, loamy garden soil into it with a dibble, butter knife, or even a chopstick. Place the plant in the crack (with the crown 2 inches in from the front of the wall, if possible), and use your tool to gently spread the plant's roots. Add more soil and then water well.

project

Espalier Apple Tree

Talk about a border that can perform multiple functions! Try your hand at the centuries-old art of espalier for a border that will bring you beauty, blossoms, and fruit that tastes nothing like those waxed orbs in the supermarket bin. Training a tree to grow in a single plane does take time and continuous pruning, but it's a rewarding endeavor that even a beginning gardener will enjoy.

MATERIALS

Apple trees (see Tips)
Heavy-gauge galvanized wire
Vinebolts
Bamboo
Twine

TOOLS AND SUPPLIES

Gardening spade
Pruners

TIPS

■ Apple trees for espalier must be *spur-bearing*, which means their fruit forms close to the main branches instead of at the tips of vertical growth. Trees with M9 dwarfing rootstock are the most suitable for espalier.

■ You'll need two varieties of apple trees on your property to facilitate cross-pollination. Ask the nursery where you purchase the tree you plan to espalier to recommend another variety to plant to provide cross-pollination.

■ The training of your tree will be easiest if you start with a whip—this is a young tree consisting of a single vertical stem without branches or side shoots.

■ All cuts should be made ¼ inch above a bud, at a 45° angle that slopes away from the bud. This allows water run-off and helps prevent disease.

INSTRUCTIONS

1 Attach horizontal heavy-gauge galvanized wires to vinebolts screwed into your wall or fence. The vinebolts should hold the wires 6 inches away from the wall or fence to allow for air circulation and pruning. Position the lowest wire 16 to 18 inches above the ground; the remaining wires should be spaced about 20 inches apart. (Wires can be strung between wooden posts for a free-standing espalier.)

2 Use the gardening spade to dig a hole 5 inches deeper than your tree's root ball, 6 to 12 inches out from the wall or fence and in the center of the horizontal wires. Add a little of the soil back into the hole, and then insert the tree. The tree's graft union (the swollen area where

the rootstock and the whip meet) should be 2 to 3 inches above ground level. Use the excavated soil to refill the hole halfway, and then water thoroughly. Adjust the tree, if necessary, so it's standing straight and its graft union is at the proper height. Allow the water to drain; then fill the hole to the top with the remaining soil. Tamp down the soil, and then water thoroughly once again.

3 To preserve moisture and prevent weed growth, spread a 3-inch layer of mulch around the tree, taking care to keep the mulch several inches away from the trunk. Water well (every three to five days) for the first month, and then water weekly for the first one or two growing seasons.

4 **FIRST WINTER:** Find a bud that's a few inches below the bottom wire and use the anvil pruners to cut the whip just above that bud (see figure 1). A shoot that will become the tree's central leader will grow from this bud, and lateral shoots will grow from buds below this one.

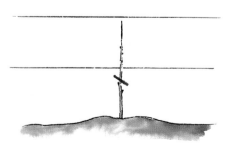

FIGURE 1. First winter

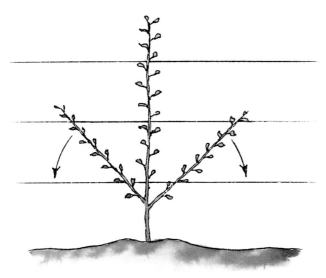

FIGURE 2. First growing season

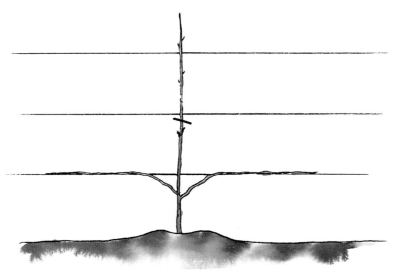

FIGURE 3. Second winter

5 **FIRST GROWING SEASON:** In early spring, use the twine to tie the central leader to the wires in a upright, vertical, position. Choose two of the lateral shoots below the central leader that appear to be healthy and equal in growth. Tie these shoots to the wires at diagonals (as shown in figure 2). Attaching them diagonally, instead of horizontally, will encourage them to grow vigorously. Throughout the summer, prune all other shoots on the tree back to two or three leaves. At the end of the growing season, bend these lateral branches very gently until you can attach them to the bottom horizontal wire. Don't ever bend a branch so that its tip is lower than the point where it attaches to the trunk, or its growth will be slowed dramatically.

6 **SECOND WINTER:** Cut the central leader to a bud just below the second wire (see figure 3). Any extra growth that was cut back to two or three leaves can now be cut back all the way to the trunk.

7 **SECOND GROWING SEASON:** In early spring, continue training the central leader vertically. Choose two healthy and equally vigorous lateral shoots growing below where the central leader was cut and attach them diagonally to the wires. Throughout the summer, prune all other lateral shoots on the tree back by two-thirds. Any shoots growing on the bottom horizontal branches should be pruned back to two or three leaves. If a horizontal branch is not growing well, return it to the diagonal position until it's caught up to its partner on the other side of the tree. At the end of the growing season, bend the second set of branches very gently until you can attach them to the second horizontal wire.

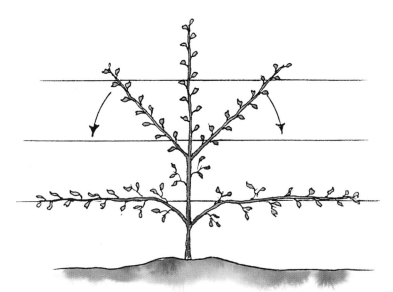

FIGURE 4. Second growing season

8 **THIRD WINTER:** Cut the central leader to just below the third wire. Lateral shoots that were cut by two-thirds during the growing season can now be cut all the way back to the trunk.

9 Continue choosing lateral shoots to train first diagonally and then horizontally until the espalier has filled its allotted space. Upright growth on the horizontal branches should be pruned so it remains below the overhead branch.

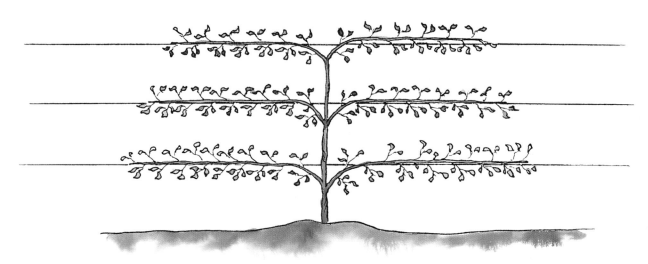

FIGURE 5. Completed espalier

Enhancing Borders

chapter

WHILE THE SIGHT OF A BRIGHTLY COLORED and extravagantly decorated garden wall might strike us as bold and contemporary, such gestures have, in fact, graced gardens since ancient times. A Roman in the first century A.D. would find nothing shocking about a hedge trimmed into the shape of an animal or a wall embedded with intricate mosaics. It is we modern homeowners who are shy about the use of color and ornamentation in the garden. Which really is a shame because a little paint, bits of broken crockery, or whimsical castoffs headed for the landfill can all be put to wonderful use enhancing borders.

Perhaps those intimidating Latin plant names, reminding us of school, lead us to think of garden design as a test we'll pass or fail, with little room for fun. Why not have a sense of humor about it? Nature (as you'll discover if you garden for any amount of time) certainly does.

Finishes

Our reticence regarding color for borders isn't due to any lack of products. A quick trip to a home improvement center will show you a dizzying selection of paints and stains suitable for outdoor use. Of course, most stone and brick walls are far too handsome to be painted; save this option for cement or cinder block walls, and use an exterior grade paint recommended for use on masonry (check to see if you need to use a special primer first). But most wooden fences must be protected from the elements with some kind of finish.

Before this finish is applied, old walls and fences should be clean and dry. (Borders with flaking or cracked paint also need to be scraped and sanded first; be alert to the possibility of lead paint on old walls and fences.) Scrub or mop old walls and fences with a mix of ½ cup of trisodium phosphate dissolved in 2 gallons of warm water. (Increase the amount of trisodium phosphate to 1 cup and add up to a pint of bleach if you're trying to remove mildew.) Rinse the border well with warm water, and allow it to dry completely. You might want to look into renting a pressure washer for large jobs. Make sure you understand how to use one properly so you don't damage your border's surface, and plan on several extra days of drying time before applying a finish.

TOP: Stains both protect and enhance a wood fence.

RIGHT: Stains can add color while still allowing the beauty of the wood to show through.

WATER SEALERS

Water sealers are usually clear finishes that offer protection without significantly altering the appearance of the wood (most wood will darken slightly once sealed). To be effective, water sealers need to be reapplied as often as once a year.

STAINS

Stains, which can be applied directly to the wood without a primer coat, come in a variety of shades and colors. You can use one that will barely alter the appearance of your wood, or you can apply an opaque stain that will give practically the same effect as paint. If you want color but would also like the wood grain to show through, then a translucent stain will fit the bill. Just make sure that whatever stain you choose is graded for exterior use and contains a sealer. Because stains actually penetrate the wood, rather than form a film on top as paint does, they are more effective for rough-surfaced fences. Stained fences also require less surface preparation when the time comes for re-staining—typically every five years.

PAINT

Tom Sawyer thought he had it bad whitewashing that picket fence, but think if he had to stand around in the aisle of a modern home improvement store while Aunt Polly chose from among the thousands of shades of paint now available! Add to the pre-mixed choices the option of a custom-mixed color that's been computer-matched to, say, your favorite poppy, and then throw in the choice of high-gloss, satin, or flat sheen, and a simple coat of whitewash will start to seem like a splendid idea.

Paint is the product that will give the most finished look to your border, and it will hide flaws better than stains or sealers. But new wood (and some masonary, too) requires a coat of primer first, matched to both the surface and the paint. The primer and the paint both need to be exterior grade, of course; check to make sure any product you intend to use on a wall is labeled for use with masonry. Reapplying paint is easiest if you do it on a regular basis—before the last coat has had time to crack or flake. Latex (water-based) paints, which tend to be easier to apply and clean up and are more environmentally benign than oil-based paints, are constantly being reformulated to stand up to the out-of-doors.

Paint hides flaws better and gives a more uniform finish than stains or sealers.

Color

Introducing color to your yard is great fun, but it can also be fairly intimidating. Let's face it: painting an entire fence or wall an unusual color will have an impact on your landscaping (not to mention your standing in the neighborhood) that can't be taken lightly. Some communities have laws that restrict the colors you can paint the street side of a wall or fence, and painting a beautiful stone or brick wall would be practically criminal. But once you've committed yourself to the idea of painting your border, you might as well be bold. If you hate it, you can always paint over it.

On the other hand, it's foolhardy to count on those color sample cards in the stores to give you a true picture of how a color will look in your yard. Buy the smallest quantity possible of the shade you're considering, paint a board or piece of plywood with it, and set it by the fence or wall you'll be painting. Pay attention to how the color looks at different times of day and from different spots in your yard. Keep in mind that the color will also be affected by the changes in sunlight and in the landscape at different times of year.

ABOVE: This playfully colored fence separates lawn from meadow.

RIGHT: Color, texture, and form all work together in this desert garden

Color and texture again play key roles in this sun-baked desert garden.

Remember, too, that color can influence moods and even our perception of distance. Greens and blues calm and relax us, while reds and oranges stimulate and excite. Blue also makes objects recede and appear smaller; a blue fence at the rear of the yard will make the yard look bigger. A white border will appear to be closer and larger. Ask yourself ahead of time what you'd like to accomplish in that part of your yard. Is your goal to jazz up a boring concrete block wall or create a private alcove for relaxation? Try not to let fashion dictate your color choice—fashions will fade faster than your paint, and there's no point in using a color you don't genuinely like. Let your plants, your house, and elements in the native landscape influence you when choosing border colors.

Veneers

If your budget calls for concrete block, but your heart is set on brick or stone, you might want to add a veneer to your wall. Veneers of simulated or real stone or brick can (depending on the quality of the product) give the appearance of a solid stone or brick wall. Veneers that use real stone or brick are usually mortared to a wall that has had masonry ties inserted as it was constructed—typically a job for a professional. But simulated veneers, which are lighter in weight and attach to walls with mortar or adhesive, are relatively easy to apply. Just make certain that you purchase a product intended for exterior use.

Techniques for Aging Wood and Stone

If you own an old house and an established garden, a brand spanking new fence or wall may look out of place. Time will, of course, eventually take care of this problem, but you can jump-start the aging process with a few techniques to speed things along. Bleaching oils and stains can be used to turn new wood the soft gray color of weathered wood. These products take about six months to accomplish what nature would need a few years to do. However, there is a price to pay for this convenience   bleaching formulas are harmful to your plants and to the environment. Use them with extreme caution, or consider letting the elements do the job for you. An alternative would be to paint the fence with a semi-transparent stain containing gray or white pigment.

If you have a stone or brick wall that faces north or gets shade for a good part of the day, you can grow moss or lichens on it to give it an aged appearance. You can simply use a paintbrush to spread a coat of yogurt or buttermilk on the surface, or if you have some moss growing already, you can try the following recipe: Take a handful of moss, a pinch of sugar, and a can of stale beer (you may substitute buttermilk for the beer), and combine them in a blender. Paint this brew on your stones or bricks; it won't look pretty and it won't smell good, but if the conditions are right, your wall should soon be wearing a distinguished coat of moss.

ABOVE: Moss and lichen soften the appearance of this north-facing stone wall.

OPPOSITE, TOP: The stucco surface of this wall mimics adobe, a natural choice for this Southwestern garden.

OPPOSITE, BOTTOM: Stucco has been used to soften the outlines of this handsome wall and entryway.

Stucco

Stucco has been used since ancient times as a protective and decorative coating on structures. It can be applied to brick or cement walls for a finish that can vary from satiny smooth to highly textured. Stucco is made from a mixture of sand, cement, water, and sometimes lime. Typically, stucco is applied to a wall and then painted with exterior masonry paint, but powdered pigment may be added directly to the mix instead. Mastering the art of stucco (or *rendering*, as it is sometimes called) is trickier than it appears, but in the hands of an expert, this versatile finish can make ho-hum concrete block or cement walls look as if they were built from finely cut stone or adobe.

Mirrors

Why settle for one gorgeous garden when you could have two? Mirrors make delightful decorations for a wall or fence. They can make a small garden appear larger or a dead end look like the doorway to a whole other garden. Old mirrors are best (search flea markets and yard sales), since anything hung on a border will soon be weathered anyway. You may want to have a companion handy when you hang a mirror, so one person can position the mirror while the other makes sure the reflections are pleasing from various angles. A mirror placed to mimic a doorway should usually be angled back just slightly to give the effect of depth and distance in the reflected landscape.

BELOW: A properly placed mirror can give the illusion of a window into a whole other garden.

OPPOSITE, TOP: A variety of objects makes up the dazzling mosaic on this wall.

OPPOSITE, BOTTOM: Mosaics and a coat of whitewash bring a touch of the exotic to a walled garden.

Mosaics

This is another ancient form of garden decoration, and another highly adaptable one. Mosaics can make a wall look elegant, exotic, or fun and funky. Use traditional fragments of ceramic tiles to form pictures, geometric patterns, or abstract designs on your wall—or attach unconventional objects as suits your fancy. Just be sure to choose materials that can stand up to the elements. Either cement grout or a waterproof adhesive is usually used to attach the mosaic pieces. If you lack confidence in your artistic ability, it's probably wise to try this fairly permanent enhancement in small doses at first. You might even want to start by covering a terra-cotta flowerpot or a small patio table first, so you can see how mosaics work with your particular setting.

Ornaments

From the conventional wall plaques that can be found in garden and gift shops to fun and funky gelatin molds, your choice of ornaments to embellish your fence or wall need only be limited by your imagination. Birdhouses, copper-bottomed pots and pans, sconces, plant holders, and statuary can all adorn your border. House walls, which often serve as a border at one end of a patio or deck, can look depressingly bare. Ornamentation can help here—whether you go playful or subdued is up to you. Vines are also valuable here: a mix of plants and objects works best to blend the man-made with the rest of your landscape.

Don't forget finials, the traditional ornament for walls and fences. Stone spheres atop stately columns or finely turned finials on posts can transform a simple border into an elegant one. Less formal walls and fences can be topped with playful finials—birds and small animals are favorites.

ABOVE: Look around and you'll find all sorts of objects to turn into wall ornaments. Here, bird cages with a coat of bright paint enhance a boldly painted wall.

LEFT: Objects and plants combine playfully to enhance this garden's border.

Trompe L'oeil and Murals

Trompe l'oeil (French for "fool the eye") is an ancient art form; it was practiced by the Greeks as far back as the fifth century B.C. But it has always been art with a touch of whimsy and humor about it (Rembrandt's students are said to have teased the master by painting coins on his studio floor). You can use this device to paint entire scenes on a stucco garden wall or to turn ordinary cement into marble or finely dressed stone. When employing trompe l'oeil in the garden, consider the angle from which it will most often be viewed—this will help you determine the placement of shadows and highlights that give the painting its three-dimensional illusion.

Murals, of course, can be traced back as far as the cave walls painted in Lascaux, France, at least 17,000 years ago. Something about a blank vertical surface seems to prompt the human urge to create. If you long for a view of the sea or an Italian vineyard, but instead are faced with a boring solid wall, reach for your paintbrush. Bright, fanciful murals tend to look best in urban settings. Translucent glazes applied to landscape murals will give them an aged appearance.

The trompe l'oeil on this wall brings a glimpse of the country to a city patio.

Topiary

Because hedges literally *grow* into your landscape, they don't stand out the way a new wall or fence might, so you don't need to worry about "weathering" them. And let's face it, there aren't a whole lot of ways to adorn or enhance a hedge. But if you have a formal evergreen hedge, you can have a great deal of fun with topiary. (Before you grab the shears, however, stop and think about whether the constant pruning required by topiary really does fall under your definition of "fun.") Topiary is another ancient art; in the thousands of years it has been practiced, plants have been sculpted into just about every form imaginable. Along with clipping your hedge into geometric shapes or training it (usually on wire frames) into leafy animals, you can also cut arches, windows, and doorways into it.

ABOVE: Meticulously shaped hedges allow form to play a lead role in this garden.

LEFT: The playful appearance of this yew walk belies the hours of patient pruning needed to maintain the sheared shrubs.

OPPOSITE, TOP: This gate offers a friendly welcome to visitors.

OPPOSITE, BOTTOM: Much more than an afterthought, a gate can be the focal point of a border.

Gates

Constructing a gate and gateposts that will do the job for years without sagging is one of the trickiest parts of building a border. It's a job you're wise to leave to an expert or else to research in detail for your particular wall or fence. (Hedges, too, sometimes have gates and gateposts installed at a break between plants.) The fun part is deciding how your gate will interact with the rest of the border. Gates with unassuming temperaments blend right in and are practically indistinguishable from the fences that surround them. Stylish gates announce their presence by

taking the architecture of a fence or wall and embellishing it or varying it slightly. Then there are the extroverts of gates. These stand apart visually from the rest of the border and shout their greetings in bright colors or bold designs.

Whatever personality of gate appeals to you, its size, placement, and direction of swing will all require careful consideration. This is not the place for shoddy hardware or sloppy construction—the gate is the part of your border that will shake hands with your guests, and no one appreciates a limp handshake.

metric conversion

Inches	Centimeters
⅛	3 mm
¼	6 mm
⅜	9 mm
½	1.3
⅝	1.6
¾	1.9
⅞	2.2
1	2.5
1¼	3.1
1½	3.8
1¾	4.4
2	5
2½	6.25
3	7.5
3½	8.8
4	10
4½	11.3
5	12.5
5½	13.8
6	15
7	17.5
8	20
9	22.5
10	25
11	27.5

Inches	Centimeters
12	30
13	32.5
14	35
15	37.5
16	40
17	42.5
18	45
19	47.5
20	50
21	52.5
22	55
23	57.5
24	60
25	62.5
26	65
27	67.5
28	70
29	72.5
30	75
31	77.5
32	80
33	82.5
34	85
35	87.5
36	90

acknowledgments

The author wishes to thank the following people for their generous help with this book:

CHRIS BRYANT, for magically transforming photos and text into a beautiful book.

DON OSBY, for his wonderful illustrations, help above and beyond the call of duty, and endless patience.

RICHARD FREUDENBERGER, for his expert technical contributions.

DEAN RIDDLE, for allowing us to show his beautiful stick and woven willow fences and telling us how he built them.

VERONIKA ALICE GUNTER and her assistants, Roper Cleland and Emma Jones, for cheerfully and competently completing every task put before them.

VAL ANDERSON for her sharp eye and expert proofing skills.

The following landscape architects generously allowed us to feature photographs of their work:

J. DABNEY PEEPLES, ARTHUR CAMPBELL, and **GRAHAM A. KIMAK** of J. Dabney Peeples Design, Associates, Inc., Easley, SC

SIGNE NIELSON, Signe Nielsen Landscape Architect, P.C., New York, NY

JANE O'NEAL SPECTOR, JOS Landscape Architect, Newton, PA

Thanks to the following homeowners for allowing us to photograph their wonderful examples of walls, fences, and hedges:

DR. JULIE NEWBURG and **PATRICK BRALICK,** Liberty, SC; **GAY** and **STEWART COLEMAN,** Biltmore Forest, NC; **HEDDY FISCHER** and **RANDY SHULL,** Asheville, NC; **DR. PETER** and **JASMINE GENTLING,** Asheville, NC; **CAROL HIRE,** Asheville, NC; **BILL AND PAT KUEHL,** Asheville, NC; **ED** and **TRENA PARKER,** Biltmore Forest, NC; Julia Nash; **PAUL** and **HAZEL SANGER,** "Carlsbad," Highlands, NC; **MARY SHELDON,** Asheville, NC; **MR.** and **MRS. GLEN** and **JAN SPEARS,** Greenville, SC; **JODI TUURI,** Asheville, NC; **SANDRA WALLACE** and **ROGER DEAN CAMP,** Asheville, NC

photo credits

WALPOLE WOODWORKERS Walpole, MA; (800) 343-6948 supplied the photographs of the beautiful fences found on pages 13 (top and bottom), 20, 51, 52, 53, 54, 57, 59, 70, and 108.

KEYSTONE RETAINING WALL SYSTEMS Minneapolis, MN; (800) 747-8971, supplied the photographs of the walls on pages 27 and 39.

The bamboo fence on page 58 was constructed and photographed by **DAVID FLANAGAN,** Bamboo Fencer, Inc., 179 Boylston St., Jamaica Plain, MA 02130; (617) 524-6137

DR. ARNOLD R. ALANEN: 29

RICHARD BABB: 11, 114 (top)

EVAN BRACKEN: 12, 18, 28, 42

WALTER CHANDOHA: 27(bottom), 33, 112, 121 (bottom)

ALAN & LINDA DETRICK: 61 and 76

DEREK FELL: Cover, 2, 5, 17, 22, 23, 60, 78, 82, 92, 95, 100, 101 (bottom)

DENCY KANE: Back cover (center right) , 5, 6, 8, 15, 48, 50, 67, 72, 81, 84, 88, 91, 98 (bottom), 99, 103, 116 (top), 124 (top)

RICHARD HASSELBERG: 3, 10 (bottom), 14, 16, 21 (all), 24, 45, 55, 56, 85, 96, 98 (top), 101 (top), 102 (bottom), 105, 107, 118, 122 (bottom), 125 (top)

CHARLES MANN: back cover (lower left and center right, 10 (top), 21 (lower left), 25, 26 (top and bottom), 80, 102 (top), 104, 106, 113 (bottom), 114 (bottom), 115, 116 (bottom), 117, 119 (top and bottom), 120, 121 (top), 122 (top), 124 (bottom), 125 (bottom)

JANE O'NEAL SPECTOR: 19

SIGNE NIELSEN: 123

index